LUTHER'S FORTRESS

ALSO BY JAMES RESTON JR.

To Defend, To Destroy, A Novel, 1971

The Amnesty of John David Herndon, 1973

The Knock at Midnight, A Novel, 1975

The Innocence of Joan Little: A Southern Mystery, 1977

Our Father Who Art in Hell:
The Life and Death of the Rev. Jim Jones, 1981

Sherman's March and Vietnam, 1985

The Lone Star: The Life of John Connally, 1989

Collision at Home Plate:
The Lives of Pete Rose and Bart Giamatti, 1991

Galileo: A Life, 1994

The Last Apocalypse: Europe at the Year 1000 A.D., 1998

Warriors of God: Richard the Lionheart and
Saladin in the Third Crusade, 2001

Dogs of God: Columbus, The Inquisition,
and the Defeat of the Moors, 2005

Fragile Innocence: A Father's Memoir of
His Daughter's Courageous Journey, 2006

The Conviction of Richard Nixon: The Untold Story
of the Frost/Nixon Interviews, 2007

Defenders of the Faith: Christianity and Islam Battle for
the Soul of Europe, 1520–1536, 2009

The Accidental Victim: JFK, Lee Harvey Oswald,
and the Real Target in Dallas, 2013

LUTHER'S FORTRESS

Martin Luther and His Reformation Under Siege

J A M E S   R E S T O N   J R .

BASIC BOOKS
A Member of the Perseus Books Group
New York

Published by Basic Books,
A Member of the Perseus Books Group

Books published by Basic Books are available at special discounts for bulk purchases in the United States by corporations, institutions, and other organizations. For more information, please contact the Special Markets Department at the Perseus Books Group, 2300 Chestnut Street, Suite 200, Philadelphia, PA 19103, or call (800) 810-4145, ext. 5000, or e-mail special.markets@perseusbooks.com.

Set in 12 point Goudy Old Style

Library of Congress Cataloging-in-Publication Data

Reston, James, Jr., 1941–
Luther's fortress : Martin Luther and his Reformation under siege /
James Reston, Jr.—First [edition].
        pages   cm
Includes bibliographical references and index.
ISBN 978-0-465-06393-2 (hardcover)—ISBN 978-0-465-05797-9 (ebook)
1. Luther, Martin, 1483–1546. 2. Reformation. I. Title.
BR326.6.R47 2015
284.1092—dc23
[B]   2014049254

10 9 8 7 6 5 4 3 2 1

for
Reverend James Ashton Devereux

CONTENTS

PROLOGUE

THIS IS THE STORY OF THE MOST INTENSE AND PIVOTAL PERIOD in the life of the great Reformer Martin Luther: the period from April 1521 to March 1522, when he was held in solitary confinement in the imposing castle called the Wartburg, after defending himself against the charge of heresy at the Diet of Worms. Months earlier, the Vatican had officially proclaimed him to be a heretic. At that conclave in Worms, through the so-called Edict of Worms, the Holy Roman emperor, Charles V, conferred double jeopardy on Luther by levying the most serious charge of the secular world against him, banning him as an outlaw. In the succeeding eleven months, Luther hid in terror, as the fear of being found and seized and eventually burned at the stake tormented him.

Like Luther's life, his movement also hung by a thread during this fraught period. His cohorts at the epicenter of the rebellion in Wittenberg, men who had rallied to his cause in the preceding years and whom the Vatican had also excommunicated, grew increasingly reckless in his absence, as Luther's time at the Wartburg wore on. If he perished, internal discord almost certainly would have undermined his movement. Luther and Lutheranism could easily have become an obscure footnote in history. At this great turning point in the history of Western civilization, the Protestant Reformation might never have happened at all.

At the Wartburg, beset by inner demons and physical torment, thrown back on his inner resources in secrecy and in solitude, the great Reformer could well have gone crazy. Instead, he wrestled courageously with the most profound questions of Christian life: priestly vows, celibacy, sexuality, priestly marriage, Heaven and Hell, obedience and dissent, ecclesiastical authority, and personal witness. He interpreted Holy Scripture for the common person. He pondered a Christianity devoid of papal guidance, fashioned a new scriptural doctrine, and reformulated biblical texts, all the while struggling at a distance to keep his fragile movement alive, vibrant, and safe from daunting external threat and internal dissension. Miraculously, Luther not only survived this ordeal at the Wartburg but flourished.

His literary output in these furtive months was astonishing: letters, sermons, essays, translations. He accomplished all of this even though he was suffering from physical ailments, and even though visions of a dire fate, hallucinations of Hell and Satan, and nightmares about his personal sinfulness troubled his mind. Indeed, without books to refer to during this period, he would succeed in changing the German language forever, as he would transform a rebellion against Rome into a lasting alternate religion.

Luther's burst of passion and brilliance—and his amazing concentration—would save his movement, impart to it a doctrine separate from Roman Catholicism, and give birth to Protestantism. Luther's accomplishments during this period catapulted him from the status of a lowly monk on the fringes of religious life in Europe to the pinnacle of Christian thought. Hounded into the Wartburg, he emerged with the strength and stature to face his persecutors—and triumph over them.

THE PERIOD OF 1483 TO 1546, LUTHER'S LIFESPAN, WAS AN era of giants: Henry VIII in England; Francis I in France; Charles V, the Holy Roman emperor presiding over most of Europe; the Medici popes, Leo X and Clement VIII in Rome; and Suleyman the Magnificent in Constantinople. It was a time of conflict between Charles V and Francis I in Italy, the sack of Rome in 1527 by Protestant forces from Germany, and the siege of Vienna by Suleyman in 1529 and 1532, when the Ottoman sultan threatened to spread the dominion of Islam all the way to the Rhine River. It was the time of Christopher Columbus and the opening of the New World, of Vasco da Gama and the opening to India, and of the Renaissance with its luminaries: Michelangelo, Leonardo da Vinci, Raphael, Albrecht Dürer, and Machiavelli.

Luther's lifetime also saw the ascendancy of some of the most powerful and interesting popes Christendom had ever known. After the glorious celebration of the Christian Jubilee in the year 1500, Julius II was elected in 1503 and became known as the warrior pope, as he presided over the reconquest of Bologna and other important papal dominions in central Italy in his effort to prevent French and Venetian domination there. But his most lasting contribution was to order the destruction of the decrepit old basilica of St. Peter's, the church of the popes, and to commission a monumental new building. Following the design of Donato Bramante, the new St. Peter's Cathedral was meant to be "a basilica that will take precedence over all the churches on earth and guarantee the security of the Christian religion."

It is this colossal project, and the way the Vatican proposed to pay for it, that is central to the Luther story.

One

THE BIRTH OF A CONTRARIAN

Martin Luther was born in November 1483 in Eisleben, a town in the German province of Saxony-Anhalt at the heart of the Holy Roman Empire. His stern father, Hans, spent his early working life deep in the copper mines of Eisleben and Mansfeld, where the groans of the mountain played tricks with men's minds, where the danger of a mine collapse or explosion was a constant worry, and where injury and death were common. Miners of the time put their trust in the mother of the Virgin Mary, St. Anne, for it was said that she never greeted her supplicants with empty hands but always brought "mighty goods and money." It was she who watched over miners' health and well-being. And when an accident happened, it was not fate but the work of the Devil, the prince of death, and he was vibrantly feared.

Satan was a constant presence for medieval Europeans. He was thought to be endlessly clever and inventive not only in spreading mayhem and despair but also in hatching tricks and pranks with which to torment the unwary. "The Devil vexes and harasses the workmen in mines," Luther would say later. "He makes them think they have found fine new veins of silver when they have labored and labored, but this turns out to be just illusions."

If supernatural forces haunted his father, Luther's mother saw evil spirits behind every curtain. Children were especially vulnerable to their charms and snares. Luther remembered a pastor from his childhood who made the mistake of punishing a witch for charming children, only to have a spell cast on him, whereupon the poor fellow fell sick and died. Children had to be wary of strange noises in the wind or in the roils of rushing waters. They were cautioned against going too deep into dark forests, especially marshy places, where evil spirits lurked in many forms and stalked the unsuspecting intruder. The Devil frequently disguised himself as bugs and caterpillars; the caterpillar was particularly suspect, for the worm was the "emblem of the Devil" in the way it crawled and changed color. The Devil not only took the shape of insects and serpents that could kill you or cause you to be killed. He was a skillful murderer who had more poisons than all the world's chemists put together. But he could also take on seemingly cuddly forms like the silly sheep that would lie and deceive you.

The world, in short, was a very scary place.

In 1491 the family moved to the nearby town of Mansfeld, where Hans Luther prospered, becoming both the owner of several copper smelters and a respected town councilor. Young Luther was educated in Latin in religious schools in Mansfeld and the Thuringian town of Eisenach, in the shadow of the famous and imposing Wartburg Castle, the very place where, some thirty years later, Luther would seek refuge from the human forces purporting to represent the Christian God. He was said to be a cheery boy, fond of singing, in love with music, and proficient in playing the lute.

In 1501 he matriculated in the traditional course in the arts at the oldest and most distinguished university in Germany at Erfurt. In the sixteenth century Erfurt was the fourth largest town in the German-speaking world, with a population of twenty-four thousand, twice as large as Frankfurt and Leipzig; its university had the largest student body in central Europe. As a student he was known as a great talker, earning the nickname "the Philosopher." In 1505 he received his degree and then, much to the satisfaction of his father, who was now a prominent burgher, Martin began a graduate course in the law.

On July 2, 1505, however, during a long sojourn in the countryside, Luther, now twenty-one, was caught in a ferocious thunderstorm on a back road near the village of Stotternheim. Terrified and cowering beneath a tree, he cried out for deliverance to St. Anne, as the copper miners had always done, and spontaneously proclaimed that if he survived the storm, he would become a monk. When he told his father of his decision, Hans Luther was furious at his son for abandoning his legal career, at least without consulting him first.

"Did you not read in Scripture that one shall honor his father and his mother?" Hans fumed.

Later, Luther would question whether his vow was sincere. In an essay in 1521 entitled "Concerning Monastic Vows," he wrote, "I did not freely or desirously become a monk, but walled around with terror and agony of sudden death, I vowed a constrained and necessary oath." Selling all his books, except Virgil and Plautus, he entered the Augustinian monastery in Erfurt twelve days after the Stotternheim thunderstorm. For the next six years Luther lived under the harsh rules of the Augustinian order. There, as time passed, he began to develop his doubts.

"I was angry with God," Luther would write. "As if it is not enough that miserable sinners are eternally lost through original sin. And that they are crushed by every kind of calamity by the law of the Decalogue. Then comes God adding pain to pain by the Gospel that threatens us with his wrath. Thus I raged . . . with a fierce and troubled conscience."

"You are a fool," his confessor said to him in response. "God is not angry with you, but you are angry with Him."

After his ordination as a priest in April 1507, he came under the paternal guidance of the vicar general of the Augustinian order, Johann von Staupitz. Von Staupitz admired Luther's gifts but worried about his ward's crippling doubts and insecurities. And so the superior took Luther under his wing as the young priest's confessor. Occasionally, these regular sessions would last many hours. Feeling that academic work might provide a healthy distraction from Luther's introspection, von Staupitz encouraged Luther to turn in that direction. In 1512 Luther received his doctorate, and as a courtesy, von Staupitz stepped aside from his chair in biblical theology at the new university at Wittenberg and gave it to Luther. In the coming few years Luther devoted himself to internal debates over the challenge of humanism and to writing essays on the fine points of scriptural doctrine. In 1514 he assumed the position of minister in Wittenberg's town church, where he became a popular preacher, especially for his ability to explain biblical stories in the simple parlance of the people.

Yet even as Luther assumed greater responsibilities within the Roman Catholic Church, his alienation from the Vatican grew, thanks in no small part to the man who had ascended to the papacy after the death of Julius II.

I N 1513, LEO X BECAME THE FIRST POPE WHO HAILED FROM THE House of Medici, the fabulous banking family of Florence. This son of Lorenzo the Magnificent was an outsized, controversial figure who styled himself as a king, and his excesses would, in time, shape Luther's opposition to the church.

After the wars and severity of Julius's reign, Leo brought to Rome the Medici focus on art, science, and literature. He had a particular interest in the classics and antiquities. Raffaello Sanzio da Urbino (Raphael) was his most important ward, and Raphael's paintings, even more than those of Michelangelo and Leonardo da Vinci (both of whom were also in Rome at this time) define the splendor of the so-called Leonine era. Before his death in April 1520, Raphael would paint the famous walls of the pope's private library, bedroom, and ceremonial space for signing documents called the Stanze. He would also complete the "cartoons" for tapestries depicting the acts of St. Peter and St. Paul. The pope commissioned these masterworks to hang in the Sistine Chapel. Raphael also decorated the *loggie*, the middle open arcade of the Vatican's three stories with classical themes. In 1515 Leo put Raphael in charge of the building of the new St. Peter's Cathedral.

Judging from Raphael's famous portrait of Leo X, now in the Pitti Palace in Florence, the pope was a man of medium height, large head, full face, and snow-white hands. His gluttony was well-known, and the pope's corpulence was on display. Raphael had his subject seated, wearing the short red cape known as a *mozetta* and the red, ermine-fringed cap known as a *camauro*, holding a magnifying glass, since Leo was shortsighted and nearly blind in one eye. An elaborately adorned bell rests next to an illuminated manuscript, accenting the pope's interest in the arts and literature.

If the visual arts flourished in these years, so did literature. It was said that more than a hundred poets hovered around the Vatican court and at their gathering place in the vineyard at Trajan's Forum. Many busied themselves in writing paeans to their papal benefactor. Leo responded by showering gifts on these writers, as well as his relatives and artists.

Nepotism also flourished under Leo. After ascending to the papacy, he appointed two of his kinsmen, Giulio de Medici, age twenty, and Giovanni Angelo de Medici, age fourteen, as cardinals.

Rome welcomed the focus on the good life that Leo brought to the Eternal City. It was widely reported that upon his accession to the papal throne, Leo had remarked, "Since God had given us the papacy, let us enjoy it."

Regardless of its veracity, the comment's tone reflects Leo's proclivities. A fine musician, he was said to possess a pleasant voice, as well as an open and generous manner, and a lusty sense of fun. Well-known for his refinement and charm, he delighted in vulgar street comedies.

This pleasure in profane amusements called into question his piety and labeled him as a humanist pope. Many believed that Leo was agnostic. Once he was pope, however, he kept up the appearance of piety. Every morning he heard Mass in the small, private Chapel of San Lorenzo, another of the treasures of the Vatican Palace. More than sixty years before, it had been painted by Fra Angelico, whose commission came from another humanist pope, Nicolas V.

Among Leo's extravagant eccentricities was his attachment to a pet white elephant named Hanno, which had been a gift from King Manuel I of Portugal. Manuel had been given this exotic pet, along with two leopards and a Persian stallion, as evidence of the heroic exploits of Portugal's mariners, like Vasco da Gama, whose epic voyage down the coast of Africa and around the Cape had recently opened India to European trade. Leo was especially fond of Hanno for the animal's habit of kneeling reverently and bellowing loudly when the beast came into the pontiff's presence. When Hanno died, after extraordinary measures including a gold-laced purgative failed to revive the animal, the pope was distraught. In his sadness Leo ordered Raphael to design a memorial and to compose an ode to his fallen friend. The paean emphasized the beast's size (twelve palms) and its "human feelings" and ended with the couplet: "That which Nature has stolen away / Raphael of Urbino with his art has restored."

Inevitably, the extravagance of Leo's luxurious lifestyle taxed the Vatican's coffers. To make matters worse, France invaded Italy in 1515, taking possession of Milan and threatening the independence of the papal dominion in central Italy. Within two years the Vatican's savings were squandered, and Leo became more and more obsessed with money. How was he to wage war and finance Raphael's work and the construction of St. Peter's, stage his lavish banquets and offer indiscriminate donations to artistic flatterers and hangers-on? He turned increasingly to bankers, borrowing enormous sums at 40 percent interest.

To address his deficits, Leo X turned to the dubious practice of selling cardinalates and archbishoprics for enormous prices. On July 31, 1517, he created thirty-one new cardinals and received 300,000 ducats (or around $50 million in today's dollars) for the appointments. In receiving this windfall, he was heard to say with breathtaking cynicism, "How well we know what a profitable superstition this fable of Jesus Christ has been for us."

The beneficiaries who bought these expensive offices had, in turn, to borrow from financiers and donors, large and small, wherever they could be found. Among the most flagrant of the papal simonies came the year after Leo's accession, when he sold the archbishopric of Mainz in Germany to a profligate young noble named Albrecht of Brandenburg. The cost of the office was 21,000 gold ducats (about $3,313,000). To raise this enormous sum, Albrecht had to borrow from the most powerful and wealthy banking institution in Germany, the House of Fugger, whose wealth and power was equivalent in Germany to that of the Medici in Italy. Albrecht received permission from the Vatican to repay the banker by the sale of a clever dispensation called indulgences.

An indulgence was a form of spiritual relief for the sins of murder, polygamy, sacrilege, theft, perjury, and witchcraft. For a hefty sum, the sinner could reduce or eliminate the number of years to be spent in purgatory through papal forgiveness. By purchasing an indulgence the miscreant purportedly showed his true repentance. The gift could apply to the sins of the dead as well as the living—and to those of the poor as well as the rich. As the modern *Catholic Encyclopedia* forthrightly states: "Money was extracted from the simple-minded among the faithful by promising them perpetual happiness in this world and eternal glory in the next." By 1515 Leo set 60,000 ducats or over $7 million dollars as the quota needed per year for the construction of the Cathedral of St. Peter. The sale of indulgences became the primary source of fundraising.

Leo justified the practice of selling indulgences by arguing that a pope could remit the guilt, forgive sin, and moderate the punishment of the sinner though the "power of the keys." The concept refers to the interchange between Christ and Simon Peter in which Christ says, "Upon this rock I will build my church; and the gates of hell shall not prevail against it. And I will give unto thee the keys of the kingdom of heaven: and whatsoever thou shalt bind on earth shall be bound in heaven: and whatsoever thou shalt loose on earth shall be loosed in heaven" (Matthew 16:18–19). The symbol of Vatican City itself contains crossed keys—the keys to heaven given to Peter, the first pope, by Christ. Leo might have added that indulgences had existed for four hundred years, ever since they had been devised as the rewards for holy warriors who served the pope.

In Germany Albrecht tapped a diligent Dominican preacher named Johann Tetzel as his chief fundraiser, and the mantra of the indulgence hawker survives:

> *As soon as the gold in the casket rings*
> *The rescued soul to heaven springs.*

L UTHER WOULD COME TO DEPLORE THE RAPACIOUS EXPLOITA-
tion of indulgences, but he had not always been against the
practice. Indeed, his attitude was quite different in 1510, when
he traveled to Rome as a young friar in a delegation of Augustinians. It was to be the only trip of his lifetime to Rome.

While the dysfunction of the city and extravagance of its holy
men would make a great impression on him, he was then scarcely
the abrasive radical he would later become. Indeed, he seemed
quite ready to embrace the possibilities of indulgences. After
touring the sites and viewing such relics as the rope with which
Judas was said to have hanged himself, he found himself at the
sacred steps of the Lateran Palace. According to legend, these
were the very steps in Jerusalem that Christ had ascended to the
palace of Pontius Pilate. (They had been transported to Rome by
angels in the fourth century.)

Like a good penitent, Luther climbed them on his knees, since
the believer who did so was promised nine years indulgence for
every step, and double for the step where Christ stumbled. Later,
Luther would say about that visit that despite the "vermin and
vileness" that he witnessed in Rome, he "believed everything."
And he even expressed sorrow that he could not transfer his
credit in purgatory to his living parents. Toward the end of his
life, in 1545, Luther changed his story a bit. His pilgrimage to
Rome became a time of disillusionment. He had "gone with onions and returned with garlic," he would say. When he got to the
top step, he suddenly had doubts about the power of his crawl.
He remembered the text "The just shall live by faith." And then,
by his own account, he said to himself, "Who knows whether this
prayer avails?"

By 1517 Martin Luther was a local luminary in Wittenberg,
a respected professor of theology at the university, and a popular town preacher. On October 31 of that year, the eve of All

Saints Day—a date that stands preeminent in the history of Protestantism—Luther crafted his litany of complaint against indulgences in Ninety-Five Theses, which he tacked to the wooden door of the Imperial Church in Wittenberg.

Luther's stated purpose in crafting his revolutionary theses was "to elicit the truth," and his complaints with church doctrine and practice painted a wide canvas. His special target was the immediate atrocity of indulgences. Indulgences were invalid, he argued, because they made relief from sin and guilt a strictly financial transaction rather than an expression of genuine contrition. Purchasing an indulgence was akin to purchasing a confessional license. Sincere repentance, he believed, was free, a true gift from God. When one paid money for relief, true guilt was left untouched. Sincere repentance must be linked to "outward signs." And the pope himself had no power to release the sinner from guilt or from the penalty for his sins.

> Number 21: Those who preach indulgences are in error when they say that a man is absolved and saved from every penalty by the pope's indulgences.
>
> Number 27: They preach only human doctrines that say as soon as the money clinks into the money chest, the soul flies out of purgatory.
>
> Number 28: It is certain that when money clinks in the money chest, greed and avarice can be increased. But when the church intercedes, the result is in the hands of God alone.

In his twenty-ninth thesis Luther wondered if souls in purgatory really wanted to be redeemed. And in the fiftieth and eighty-sixth theses he turned to the link between indulgences and the building of the new St. Peter's Cathedral:

Number 50: Christians should be taught that, if the pope knew the exactions of the indulgence-preachers, he would rather the church of St. Peter were reduced to ashes than be built with the skin, flesh, and bones of the sheep.

Number 86: Since the pope's income today is larger than that of the wealthiest of wealthy men, why does he not build this one church of St. Peter with his own money, rather than with the money of indigent believers?

In short, the link between money and salvation was insidious and sacrilegious, exposing the church and the pope to ridicule, and making Christian people unhappy.

Dutifully, Luther sent a copy of his theses to the archbishop of Brandenburg and to his own bishop, as if to show that while he was a harsh critic, this was merely a lively dispute within the family. But the protest quickly spread far beyond the family. With the availability of mass printing, which had developed after the adaption of moveable type by Gutenberg sixty-seven years earlier, the document was printed in Latin and distributed across Europe.

Rome's counteroffensive was fierce. Luther's case was immediately referred to the Dominicans, the hounds of God, whose role in the church was to police and protect the purity of Catholic dogma, including, most importantly, the supreme authority of the pope over his Christian ministers. A Dominican scholar, Sylvester Prierias, the "commissioner of the Sacred Palace," was given the case, and after studying the Ninety-Five Theses, he drew up a bill of particulars that formally alleged the "suspicion of disseminating heresy."

"Just as the Devil smells of his pride in all his works," Prierias said of Luther, "so you smell of your own malevolence." The Vatican demanded that the alleged apostate come to Rome immediately to face the Inquisition.

Luther demurred, pleading illness and calling Rome "a place of hydras and portents." In frustration the Vatican sent a papal legate to Germany with the mandate to bring Luther to heel, only to discover that sympathy for Luther was wide and growing. A public disputation between Luther and the legate was held in Augsburg, only to disintegrate into a shouting match.

"Go and do not return unless you are ready to recant!" the legate shouted.

"I will not become a heretic by contradicting the opinions that made me a Christian," Luther responded. "I would rather be burned, exiled, accursed."

Even into early 1519 Luther was maintaining a correct though insincere stance in his formal communications with Rome. In a letter to the pope in March 1519, Luther wrote: "It has never been in my mind to attack the authority of the Roman Church or the Pope. On the contrary, I acknowledge that the authority of the Roman Church surpasses all other, and nothing in heaven or on earth, save only Jesus Christ, is to be put above it." Around the same time, he was writing to George Spalatin, Elector Frederick's court chaplain, saying that he couldn't decide if the pope was actually the Anti-Christ or merely his emissary.

Luther's many insults had, of course, reached the ears of the pope. Leo must have guffawed when he received Luther's deferential letter. Still, he chose to take the missive at its face, as an expression of obedience. Characteristically, in this age of Macchiavelli, Guicciardini, and Erasmus, Leo had chosen two well-known men of letters, Pietro Bembo and Giulio Sadoleto, as his personal secretaries, and they crafted papal correspondence in elegant and flowing Latin. When Luther heard about the pope's literary scribes, he remarked, "The pope selected Sadoleto for his talents to write against me. My God, may Thy light enlighten him and guide him in the right way!"

Sweet paternal forbearance perfumed the pope's reply to Luther. The pontiff was "delighted with Luther's repentant submission" and invited the monk "to set forth at once to Rome, there to make a retraction." Luther pleaded poverty as an excuse for his inability to accept the pope's invitation. The pope answered by offering to pay his expenses. Luther did not respond. If Luther now regarded the pope as the Anti-Christ, he began to refer to Rome as Babylon, the lair of the Anti-Christ, the city of evil. Romans, he said, were out to get him "by Italian subtlety, poison, or assassination." He had been slandered by children of mammon (the money-grubbers), he said, and by gluttonous misers who hungered after the milk and the wool of Christ's lamb. (Luther's constant references to gluttony in these attacks were a clear allusion to Leo's eating habits.)

This period of 1519 is widely regarded as the time when Luther turned from a mere disputant into a revolutionary. He was receiving offers of support and protection from a boisterous cadre of anti-Catholic humanists in Germany whose insults exceeded those of Luther himself. One of these agitators was Ulrich von Hutten, a militant German scholar who headed a group called Imperial Knights of the Holy Roman Empire, which was dedicated to undermining the secular influence of the church. Hutten railed against the papacy as "a gigantic blood sucking worm." In the midst of this "barnyard sits that insatiable corn weevil that devours piles of fruit," he wrote, "surrounded by many fellow gluttons, who first suck our blood and then consume our flesh, and now seek to grind our bones and devour all that is left of us. Will not the Germans take up their arms and make an onslaught on them with fire and sword?"

Meanwhile, two other Imperial Knights, Sylvester von Schaumberg and Franz von Sickingen, offered to protect Luther with soldiers. Jubilantly, Luther crowed to a fellow Augustinian that his two military supporters "have freed me from all human respect. Franz von Sickingen promises to protect me through Hutten from all my enemies. Sylvester von Schaumburg will do the same with his Franconian nobles. Now I no longer fear and am publishing a book in the German tongue about Christian reform, directed against the pope, in language as violent as if I were addressing Anti-Christ."

That book would be the third of Luther's tracts published in 1520 called *Concerning Christian Liberty*, and it carried a preface in the form of a letter to Pope Leo X. In the letter Luther refrained from calling the pope the Anti-Christ. Rather, he portrayed the pontiff as an innocent, buffeted by the waves of Rome, a Daniel in the lion's den (Daniel 6:1–28), an Ezekiel among scorpions (Ezekiel 2:6), a victim of the evil flatterers who surrounded the papal throne. "I have never consigned any evil concern to your person," he wrote disingenuously. "Instead, I desire that eternal blessing may fall to your lot." In several instances he referred to Leo as "your Blessedness," as "Leo my father," and "most excellent Leo." But while he lavished the pope with faint praise, he warned that evil men around the pope were creating mayhem in his name and implicitly without his permission. "The Church of Rome, formerly the most holy of all churches, has become the most lawless den of thieves, the most shameless of brothels, the very kingdom of sin, death and hell," Luther wrote, "so that not even the Anti-Christ, if he were to come, could devise any addition to its wickedness."

Rome was not only Babylon, Luther claimed, but Sodom. It stunk in the nostrils of the world, and papal authority was growing weak. There was nothing more pestilential, more hateful, more corrupt than the court of Rome. He warned the pope against those sirens who would make him more than merely a man, but partly a god, so that he could command whatever he would. "Let not those men deceive you, as they pretend that you are lord of the world who will not allow any one to be a Christian without your authority, who babble of your having power over heaven, hell, and purgatory." Those men were Leo's enemies, Luther wrote, and invoked Isaiah 3:12: "They that call thee blessed are themselves deceiving thee. They cause thee to err, and destroy the way of thy paths."

He, Martin Luther, was storming against this seat of pestilence. He looked upon the court of Rome with contempt and was divorcing himself from it. In this pronouncement he invoked Revelation 22:11: "He that is unjust, let him be unjust still: and he which is filthy, let him be filthy still."

Between October 1517 and late 1520, Luther's conflict with Rome widened, and his positions hardened. The Reformer brazenly challenged the most sacrosanct rituals of Catholic faith. He questioned the validity of Catholicism's seven sacraments, including marriage and extreme unction (last rites for the dying). He denied the need to lift the host skyward in the Eucharist and wondered whether it was necessary for the Christian to believe in the transformation of the bread and wine into the body and blood of Christ. He began to think of the demand of celibacy for priests as the work of the Devil. He moved toward the central tenet of his eventual doctrine, "justification by faith alone," which denied the value and necessity of good works in attaining heavenly salvation. He began to espouse a direct relationship between the believer and the Almighty without the need for intermediaries and based solely in the conscience of the supplicant. He deplored the extravagance of priestly garb in the Mass, especially as excessive pomp was manifest in Rome.

Luther was shaking the very foundations of the Roman church, not only in contesting its core beliefs but also in questioning its political power in the world. In the early sixteenth century the church was all-powerful, and one trembled in daring to question its political and moral authority. It crowned kings, conferred moral sanction on their exercise of governance, withheld its favors from those influential persons who displeased it, and decided who went to Heaven and who went to Hell. It is small wonder that these challenges drew the fire of popes and kings.

His anti-papist rhetoric grew more violent by the month, and as his rebellion spread across Germany, fueled by the revolution in mass printing, he grew bolder. His public pronouncements became more and more messianic, as he suggested that God was speaking through him to reform His church. Reconciliation became less and less conceivable.

In June 1519, another disputation, this time very public and attended by a throng, was held in Pleissenburg Castle in Leipzig. Luther's opponent was the most famous theologian in all of Germany: Dr. Johann Eck, the vice chancellor of the University of Ingolstadt. In this debate Luther did not fare so well, and in general, Eck was said to have won the fight on points. But after the encounter the academic hurried to Rome, convinced that the villain had to be crushed. Joining with the papal legate from the previous disputation, Eck and his colleague drafted a bull of excommunication. Pope Leo X joined in the bull's final polish, and it was formally presented to the college of cardinals for their approval.

ON JUNE 15, 1520, THE PAPAL BULL EXSURGE DOMINE WAS promulgated. "Arise, O Lord, and judge your cause," it began. The bull identified and condemned forty-one errors from Luther's writings and sermons. His books were to be burned—not an inconsiderable task, since between 1518 and 1520 Luther's writing had become so prolific that the number of his published titles grew from 150 to 570. If, after sixty days, the culprit did not

Bulla contra errores
Martini Lutheri
z sequacium.

Leo's Bull of Condemnation.
CREDIT: STIFTUNG LUTHERGEDENKSTÄTTEN
IN SACHSEN-ANHALT, WITTENBERG

recant, the Vatican threatened, he was to be ostracized, or better yet, seized and brought to the fire of holy justice. The bull ended with these words: "Therefore let Martin himself and all those adhering to him, and those who shelter and support him, through the merciful heart of our God and the sprinkling of the blood of our Lord Jesus Christ, know that from our heart we exhort and beseech that he cease to disturb the peace, unity, and truth of the Church. . . . Let him abstain from his pernicious errors that he may come back to us. If they really will obey, . . . they will find in us the affection of a father's love, the opening of the font of the effects of paternal charity, and opening of the font of mercy and clemency. In the meantime, we enjoin on Martin that he cease from all preaching or from all activity in the office of preacher."

"It is hoped," remarked one cardinal, "that as soon as the bull is published in Germany, most men will forsake Luther." After the bull was published, Luther's enemies conducted well-publicized, ceremonial burnings of his works in Catholic towns across Germany and Holland.

But the flames could not keep up with the distribution, and Luther's response was brusque and uncompromising.

"Farewell, thou unhappy, lost, blaspheming Rome," Luther wrote during the week the bull of excommunication was issued. "The wrath of God has come upon thee, as thou hast deserved. We have cared for Babylon, but she is not healed. Let us then leave her, that she may be the habitation of dragons, specters, and witches, and true to her name of Babel an everlasting confusion, a new pantheon of wickedness."

The proclamation had given Luther sixty days to recant his errors. Well past that deadline, on December 10, 1520, Luther led a rowdy crowd of students and supporters to the Elster Gate of Wittenberg and there, dramatically and memorably, consigned the papal bull to the flames. With a note of resignation he proclaimed, "I give myself up to the peaceful and quiet study of sacred literature, so that by this I might be of use to the brethren living about me."

His breach with Rome was now complete, irreconcilable, and permanent.

THE YEAR 1521 OPENED IN ROME WITH A REAFFIRMATION OF Luther's excommunication. On January 3, 1521, Leo X published a new bull called *Decet Romanum Pontificum* ("It Pleases the Roman Pontiff . . ."). It made the excommunication unqualified and official. All areas that supported the rebellion were put under interdict, meaning that priests there could not offer the sacraments of the church, including the Eucharist, baptism, or

Luther Burning the Papal Bull. By Paul Thurmann. CREDIT: ULRICH KNEISE, WARTBURG FOUNDATION

extreme unction. Two weeks later, on January 18, Leo X sent an urgent request to the Holy Roman emperor, Charles V, to have the bull of excommunication widely published through Germany. Charles, said the pope, would wear the sword of his authority in vain if he did not deploy his forces against infidels and heretics.

From mid-January 1521 onward, Leo X preoccupied himself almost exclusively with the German problem. Things were going from bad to worse. The papal nuncio in Germany, Girolamo Aleander, generally an optimistic voice, wrote that "nine-tenths of the German people cry 'Luther!' The other tenth shout 'Death to the Pope!'" If the pope was obsessed with Luther, he also feared

Pope Leo X. By Raphael. CREDIT: THE YORCK PROJECT

him. Yet in the early months of the year, he did his best to mask his worries.

For the time being, Rome's hope to contain the contagion rested with Charles V, the twenty-year-old Hapsburg scion who had been elected the year before. The pope had supported the candidacy of young Charles out of necessity, for he had to have Charles's help in confronting Luther. Upon the Hapsburg's election, Leo had written to the new emperor, "As there are two planets in heaven, the sun and the moon, which surpass in brilliancy all the stars, so there are two great dignitaries on earth, the pope and the emperor, to whom all other princes are subject and owe obedience." Two weeks after that, Leo wrote Charles another letter, berating himself for past leniency toward Luther. Luther's pride, he wrote, could not be "cured" with charity. The time for severity had arrived.

But the young emperor-elect wavered between his allegiance to the pope and his concern for rebellion in his German dominion. Charles stood ready to condemn Luther all right. But for political reasons, as a gesture to Luther's many passionate followers, he promised Luther a fair hearing at the forthcoming Diet of Worms in April.

Leo had a better idea. Might not the emperor grant Luther a private interview without witnesses? Should the culprit acknowledge his heresy, the emperor could promise him a papal pardon or else give him safe conduct to Rome or to the Spanish Inquisition. (Had Luther received the pope's offer of a safe conduct to the Inquisition, he would certainly have had a tart response.) If Luther did not accept such an invitation, Charles should proceed against him and his followers. If he accepted but did not recant, the campaign of burning his books should be intensified. The pope's chief assistant, his cousin Cardinal Guilio de Medici, ordered Aleander, the papal nuncio, to say to the emperor that Luther's rebellion was as much the emperor's affair as that of the Holy See, because religious "innovators" were as much interested in overthrowing the authority of the empire as the church. The young man seemed to need bucking up, so the pope turned to flattery. On February 25 Leo wrote to Charles of his pleasure at "seeing with joy that His Majesty was rivaling Constantine, Charlemagne, and Otto I in his zeal for the honor of the Church." He praised God for inspiring the emperor.

In March, as matters approached a stalemate, Charles took things into his own hands. He issued an invitation to Luther, couched in terms that would have made Leo X cringe: "To our noble, dear, and esteemed Martin Luther, both we and the Diet have decided to ask you to come to Worms under safe conduct to answer with regard to your books and teaching. You have 21 days in which to arrive."

This was more a summons than an invitation. It came from the highest secular authority, and Luther could scarcely ignore it, as he had ignored the Vatican's "invitation" to visit the Spanish Inquisition. When Luther heard it, he was pleased. "I am heartily glad that His Majesty will take to himself this affair that is not mine but that of all Christianity and the whole German nation," he wrote to a supporter. The papal nuncio could only complain that Luther's appearance at Worms would merely give the Devil a platform for his "godless doctrines."

The critical element of the invitation was the promise of safe conduct. Heavy on Luther's mind was surely the case of the erstwhile "heretic" Jan Huss a century earlier. After he had professed some of the same concepts that Luther was now espousing, Huss too had been promised protection from injury and violence on a similar journey, only to be conducted swiftly into the flames. Nevertheless, Luther's response was characteristically grandiloquent. "If I am being invited simply to recant, I will not come," he wrote to a friend. "If recanting is all that is wanted, I can do that perfectly well right here. But if he is inviting me to my death, then I will go. I hope none but the papists will stain their hands in my blood. The Anti-Christ reigns. The Lord's will be done."

The stage was thus set for an epic confrontation. Would the contagion spread, or could it be stopped? If Luther was killed, would his fragile protest be quickly forgotten as powerful church and imperial forces snuffed out the flame? If Luther somehow survived by confessing error, would he be pushed aside by the radical evangelists all around him, and the movement die in a spectacular self-immolation? And what of Luther himself? With all that was riding on his performance at Worms, and on the events afterward, what resources of inner strength did he possess?

Luther likened his suffering and his passion to Christ's, but there was a major distinction. Unlike Christ's silence before Pilate, Luther planned to be bold and loquacious before Charles.

He was eager to appear.

IVCAE · OPVS · EFFIGIES · HAEC · EST · MORITVRA · LVTHERI ·
AETHERNAM · MENTIS · EXPRIMIT · IPSE · SVAE ·
· M · D · X · X · I ·

Luther in 1521. By Lucas Cranach. CREDIT: STIFTUNG LUTHERGEDENKSTÄTTEN IN SACHSEN-ANHALT, WITTENBERG

Two

WORMS

ON PALM SUNDAY 1521, OUTSIDE HIS TOWN CHURCH IN Wittenberg, a thin, athletic Martin Luther climbed up on his simple, two-wheeled wagon and, to the assemblage of well-wishers, colleagues at the university, and brothers in his Augustinian order, proclaimed, "We see Christ suffer. . . . Christ lives, and I shall enter Worms." Dread was in the air, not merely for the safety of the group's spiritual, moral, and political leader, but also for the future of its nascent revolution. It was Luther's insight and bravado that held the dissidents together. What if he should be taken from them?

In the audience were mentors and colleagues: Philipp Melanchthon, his young alter ego and chief disciple; Andreas Karlstadt, the dean of the university faculty, who had conferred a doctorate on Luther and would later become his chief rival; and Johann von Staupitz, his greatest supporter and adviser, the head of the congregation of his order, and the priest who had nurtured him through his doubts as a young monk. All were implicated in Luther's rebellion. The papal bull had condemned not only him but all his supporters, adherents, and accomplices as "barren

Charles V, Holy Roman Emperor. By Bernaert
van Orley. Credit: The Yorck Project

vines which are not in Christ." They were all in jeopardy, especially if the emperor formally condemned their leader.

Besides his creaky conveyance, the university had provided its
beleaguered professor with twenty golden ducats and two traveling companions, one of whom was Nicholas von Amsdorf, a
theologian on the Wittenberg faculty. The Holy Roman emperor, Charles V, in turn, was providing an imperial herald to
escort the villain's caravan and enforce the emperor's promise of
safe conduct.

But was the promise sincere? There was no way to know. Luther was traveling as an excommunicant. Any true believer who felt he was following the teaching of the Apostle Paul on heretics might seize him and deliver him to the Inquisition at any point along the perilous journey to the Rhine River. Many in the crowd surely suspected that the odds of Luther making it back to Wittenberg alive were poor.

In 1521 Luther was far from the pudgy figure he would later become. His close friend, the painter Lucas Cranach, had fashioned a copper engraving of him early in that year, doffing a jaunty professor's cap, with a chiseled profile and a stylized growth of whiskers under his chin. Luther would need this fighting trim in the coming months.

His route took him south through Leipzig, where his pamphlets and books would later be churned out by the thousands on the new printing press. At each town he received a hero's welcome. In Naumburg an exuberant and somewhat dense supporter presented him with a portrait of Girolamo Savonarola, who, like Luther, had challenged and derided a pope twenty-three years earlier and had been burned at the stake for his transgressions. Luther's derision of Leo, the Holy Father, had far exceeded the apostasy of Savonarola, and his rebellion was far more dangerous to Rome. Only days earlier he had written to a friend: "This will be my recantation in Worms. Previously I said the pope is Vicar of Christ. I recant. Now I say the pope is the adversary of Christ and the apostle of the Devil."

As he spoke to ever larger crowds along the way, the Reformer compared his suffering and his passion to Christ's. His journey was a martyr's trek, akin to Christ's journey to Jerusalem, his two-wheeled wagon the equivalent of Christ's donkey. The Anti-Christ reigned, Luther told the throngs, and the emperor was his servant.

Through Weimar the procession became ever more triumphant. At Erfurt, where Luther had been invested in the Augustinian order sixteen years before, a local priest praised him for
cleansing the "filth" of the town. Hours later, in contravention
of the papal bull to cease all preaching, Luther sermonized to an
immense crowd in the Augustinian church. The church was so
packed that a balcony nearly collapsed under the weight of the
throng, forcing his admirers to jump out of the windows.

He took for his text John 20:19–21, about Jesus appearing in
the midst of his disciples the first day after his crucifixion, show-
ing them the wounds in his hands and side, and saying, "Peace
be unto you: as my Father hath sent me, even so send I you."
Luther's sermon focused on original sin and his principal theological difference with Rome: his notion of justification by faith
alone. "None of our works have any power whatever," he bel-
lowed. "They are utterly worthless. But the papal dominion treats
us altogether differently. It makes rules about fasting, praying,
and butter-eating, so that whoever keeps the commandments of
the pope will be saved and whoever does not keep them belongs
to the Devil. It seduces the people with the delusion that goodness and salvation lie in their own works. But I say none of the
saints, no matter how holy they were, attained salvation by their
works. Salvation does not lie in our own works, no matter what
they are. It cannot and will not be effected without faith."

No doubt his audience hoped he would address the coming
confrontation in Worms, but only toward the end of his sermon
did he make an allusion to it. "I must and I will tell the truth.
That's why I'm standing here," he said. Did that remark prefigure
what he would say days later before the emperor? He closed by
saying, "Remember that God has risen up for our sakes." For the
attentive, this was an unmistakable reference to the bull of excommunication, *Exsurge Domine*, "Arise God."

When he had finished, a priest and professor of Erfurt University remarked that "by the power of his mouth, hearts were melted like snow in springtime as he showed the way to heaven's treasures which have been closed to us for centuries." But after Luther's departure, his enthusiasm for Luther's performance soon cooled. The dean of St. Severin Church, a dedicated papist, immediately confronted the priest who had welcomed Luther, grabbed him by his robe, dragged him publically from the chancel, and excommunicated him on the spot. In response, students at Erfurt University protested the priest's humiliation. Their protest would explode a few weeks later, when they stormed the dean's house and torched it.

Through Gotha and Eisenach, in the shadow of a huge bastion called the Wartburg Castle, Luther seemed more and more in the grip of his passion. "I am lawfully called to appear in Worms, and thither I shall go in the name of the Lord, though there are as many Devils as tiles on the roofs there, and they are all combined against me."

He invoked Christ's journey to Jerusalem more and more. "But Christ lives," he thundered, "and we shall enter Worms through its gates of Hell." If he was brazen in public, he was tormented by anxiety in private. His body was in "ill humor," and he had to be bled in Eisenach before he felt well enough to continue his journey.

On April 16, 1521, as the steeples of the old town of Worms came into view, he rose in his chariot and, according to prominent historians of music, began to belt out the lines of a hymn that he had reportedly composed several days before in the town of Oppenheim. One can only imagine its powerful lines echoing against the walls: "A mighty Fortress is our God; a trusty shield and weapon; he'll keep us free from the ill that hath us now overtaken. The ancient, evil enemy has risen with purpose; he wears armament strong of craft and power. On earth there is no one like him." It was to become the anthem of his Reformation.

WHEN THE NEWS ARRIVED IN ROME THAT LUTHER WAS TO be heard at the Diet of Worms, there was great distress. Would this not give Luther the very pulpit he craved? Cardinal Guilio de Medici expressed his contempt: "If Charles is able to effect so little against one man who is in his power, what could the Church and Christendom expect of him in a fight against the Turks and infidels?"

At this critical juncture, when the church was being viciously attacked for its corruption and the pope himself assailed as an agnostic hedonist, Leo chose to stage a shocking pagan pageant on the night of Carnival. Baldassare Castiglione, a prominent man of letters and ambassador to Rome for the Marquis of Mantua, left a detailed description of this tawdry papal entertainment. (Castiglione is the subject of one of Raphael's most famous portraits, now in the Louvre.)

A dark green stage had been set up in the courtyard of the Castel Sant' Angelo, and the pope and his court watched from an upper window, as dancers from Siena began the show by performing a suggestive Moorish dance. Then a lovesick woman took the stage, pleading with Venus to send her a lover. At a drum roll, eight dour hermits in gray tunics emerged from the wings, with their faces covered, and then opposite them Cupid appeared with his bow and arrows. The hermits moved threateningly toward Cupid, snatching his bow, and Cupid, in tears, appealed to Venus to save him from these awful tormenters. Venus arrived heroically in the nick of time and put the hermits to sleep with a magic potion. Retrieving his bow, Cupid generously shot his arrows into the sleeping hermits, awakening them. Casting off their tunics, the hermits were transformed into handsome young men, and surrounding the woman, they all proclaimed their love for her. But she, suddenly stalwart and unimpressed, demanded a show of manliness. Weapons were drawn. In the ensuing sword play, seven of the eight were killed, and the lone survivor got the woman as his prize.

What, one wonders, would Luther have thought of such a vulgar, profane, and vaguely erotic spectacle for the amusement of the vicar of Christ?

If Lent began with such frivolity in Rome, the season ended very differently. Maundy Thursday was the traditional day for listing the enemies of the church, along with the command that bishops throughout the entire dominion of Roman Catholicism publish the list broadly. There was resistance to the tradition. In the year previous, the king of France, Francis I, had forbidden the list's publication and announced that anyone who did so "should be drowned," probably because he was a candidate for the list himself, having invaded papal domains in northern Italy. To that Guilio de Medici countered by telling the French nuncio: "The Pope thinks it better to make no reply to this threat, lest he be carried away by anger. Therefore, should the King repeat the intimidation in your presence, you must reply pleasantly that such a threat is not likely to make the Sacred College anxious to comply with further requests of his, whether it be about a cardinal's hat or anything else." (The creation of new cardinals was an important trump card in the pope's deck; Charles V and Francis I were continually hectoring the pope to appoint new cardinals of their choosing.)

On March 28, 1521, Luther's name was put on the list for the first time. When Luther heard about his latest distinction after he arrived in Worms, he received it with a sense of glee. Without delay he reprinted the proclamation in German translation, appended marginal notes, and dubbed the papal bull the "Bull of the Supper," since it could only have been written by one who was "drunk while devouring his supper." No one could miss this reference to the pope's gluttony. Routinely now, Luther gravitated to the scatological in instructing his followers about papal commandments. Just as papal decretals or official pronouncements by the pope should be regarded as "the excrement of his holiness," so this latest papal insult should be viewed in the same way as one viewed "the poop in front of you in the street."

As Luther was making his way to Worms in his rickety wagon, the pope in the splendor of his Vatican apartments was doing his best to mask his anxiety. On April 3, he wrote to Charles's ambassador in Rome, Juan Manuel: "Thank God that He has given to me at this time an Emperor who has the Church at heart." But the pope was not so sure of the emperor's moral fiber. On April 8 Manuel sent a special courier to Worms, emphasizing the pope's impatience and hunger for news. Surely Luther must have arrived in Worms by then.

LUTHER'S ENTRANCE INTO WORMS ON APRIL 16, 1521, WAS grand. Surrounded by outer and interior defensive walls, the city was divided by a broad promenade called Kämmerstrasse, the "street of offices." Despite the efforts of the papal nuncio and the imperial authorities to discourage a public spectacle, the boulevard was alive with spectators, as Luther's simple wagon entered the town, escorted by the imperial herald on horseback. On the escort's doublet hung the imperial eagle, signifying Luther's safe conduct.

Some two thousand onlookers lined the street. Copies of the Reformer's latest pamphlets were held high, including the three major treatises he had published in 1520 that equated the pope with the Anti-Christ, questioned the basis of the seven sacraments of the medieval church, and laid down what the Catholic Church would later dub "a sensualized code of matrimonial ethics." A special press had been set up in Worms solely for the purpose of churning out his tracts and distributing them to the throng.

When Luther reached the house of the military monks known as Knights Hospitaller, he played to the crowd.

"God will be with me," he cried brazenly. "I am ready to jump into the mouth of the Behemoth."

Immediately, dukes and princes sought him out. One randy knight, from whatever prurient instinct, heckled him about his shocking assertion that a wife with an impotent husband was free to find a more virile man, perhaps her husband's brother. Luther waved the question aside as an impertinent irrelevance. The villainy of the pope was the only question at issue.

The following morning, again snubbing his nose at the papal ban, Luther reverted briefly to his role as a simple village monk and heard the confession of an ailing, aged elector. And then, without warning, his body shook with severe panic. He fell to the ground in prayer and supplication and raw terror. Suddenly he doubted the worth of his mission and wondered if his God had deserted him.

"Oh Almighty and Everlasting God," he cried, "how terrible is the World! Behold! It opens its mouth to swallow me up. I have so little trust in Thee. My last hour is come. My condemnation has been proclaimed." His work, he pleaded, was not his but God's. He had been chosen to do this. "Then stand by my side. I am ready to lay down my life for Thy truth."

Later in the day, at the appointed time, guards escorted him through back alleys to avoid the crowds to the auditorium next to the imposing High Romanesque Cathedral of St. Peter. The anticipation was electric. In the auditorium packed with delegates the noble young emperor sat grandly on a raised dais, the symbol of his power, the imperial eagle, above his head. He was dressed in a velvet cloak and soft hat. He leaned forward, his distinctive Hapsburg chin jutting forward, as Luther was led into the hall.

The scene was as foreign to Charles as it was to Luther. The twenty-one-year-old monarch had been raised in the Netherlands and spoke no German. He had only succeeded to the vast Hapsburg inheritance with his coronation as the Holy Roman emperor in Aachen the previous October. He seemed uncertain of himself and more than a little wary of the monk standing before him. To a retainer he whispered bravely in French,

"This fellow will never make a heretic out of me."

By the emperor's side stood the papal nuncio, Cardinal Girolamo Aleander, decked out in his brilliant red regalia and sporting his distinctive cardinal's biretta. For months Aleander had labored to prevent this spectacle: he feared the Reformer's eloquence and contempt for both secular and clerical authority. He worried that the proceeding would only fuel the rebellion Luther had inspired. The cardinal himself had drafted the bull of excommunication. In it he had labeled Luther the new Porphyry, comparing him to the fourth-century slanderer who had vilified Jesus as a criminal, who wrote that Jesus was justly condemned for his crime against the Roman state, and who claimed the Savior was unworthy of the hero's status conferred on him by misguided followers. It had then been the cardinal's thankless task to bring Luther's formal condemnation to Germany. There he had been humiliated and even jostled for his troubles.

Aleander had pleaded with the emperor simply to proclaim an imperial ban on Luther, to couple it with the Vatican's excommunication. Sacred and profane authority would then be joined, and justice would be done. But the emperor had feared a political backlash if Luther was not given a fair hearing, which Charles had promised at his investiture as emperor.

Now Cardinal Aleander would try to limit the proceeding to two simple questions. A simple yes or no was all that was required or that would be allowed. This was not a disputation. The Diet of Worms was not to have the appearance of an ecclesiastical council. The "satanic dragon" was to be denied a stage to spew his filth. That goal was clear. The actual interrogation of Luther was handed over to Dr. Johann Eck, the theologian who had bested Luther in their disputation in Leipzig nearly two years earlier.

On a side table Luther's works lay in a pile. An inventory of the scurrilous oeuvre was presented to the emperor. "Let them read the titles!" someone shouted out in anger, and it was done, one by one. Silence was called for, and the inquisitor stepped forward to take charge.

"Martin Luther!" Eck boomed. "His Majesty has ordered you to be called hither to retract the books that bear your name and have been spread abroad. I refer to all these books either in German or Latin." Did Luther write these books?

Suddenly, the witness seemed to lose his courage and became uncharacteristically unsure of himself. "The books are mine," he answered softly. "And I have written more." As the princes and prelates pressed closely around him, straining to hear his whispers, Luther appeared overwhelmed. He began to sweat profusely. The second question came without delay. Did he wish now to retract their contents? Would he recant the pernicious poison of his errors?

After a long pause, the Reformer spoke: "This touches God and His Word. . . . "

The delegates leaned forward, their hands to their ears. What did he say? His words were barely audible.

"This affects the salvation of souls," the witness stammered. "Christ said, 'He who denies me before men, him will I deny before my Father.'" The humble monk would dare to compare himself to Christ? Grumbles of discontent greeted this impudence. "To say too little or too much would be dangerous," he continued. "I beg you give me more time."

Luther at Worms. Credit: Stiftung Luthergedenkstätten in Sachsen-Anhalt, Wittenberg

Disbelief filled the hall. Was this man not famous for his eloquence? Had he not had three weeks to consider his defense? Amid the commotion the emperor was befuddled. What had Luther said? Luther was asked to repeat his answer in Latin.

Of all those in the packed hall, the most astonished, the most disappointed, and even the angriest were Luther's own supporters. How much they had invested in this man! Was he faltering at the most critical moment? This was no time to become faint-hearted. The implications were profound. The monk was hustled out. Twenty hours were granted for him to consider his answer.

THE SENSATIONAL NEWS OF LUTHER'S FAILURE OF NERVE raced through the town. The public frenzy was uncontrollable. A larger hall had to be commandeered for the next day's proceedings. On the morning of April 18 it filled up so quickly and was so crowded that only the emperor could sit.

When Luther entered the hall this time, his demeanor was utterly transformed. Again the delegates pressed in around him. Again the emperor leaned forward, straining to get a sense of the Reformer's guttural speech. Again the inquisitor, Dr. Eck, asked his essential question.

"Are you prepared to defend all that your writings contain, or do you wish to retract all or any part of them?"

In a strong, confident voice now the Reformer began with what sounded like a supercilious mock apology. "I ask pardon," he said, "if by reason of my ignorance, I am wanting in the manners that befit this court. I was not brought up in king's palaces, but in the seclusion of a cloister." In this company of nobles, this preamble seemed to level the field. *Their* power came accidentally from inheritance and wealth, their manners from breeding. *His* power flowed solely from his conscience.

Should Luther retract his writings? He joined the issue immediately and parsed the matter in three parts. Yes, he had written from the stance of a devout Christian and theologian. Even his adversaries, nay, even the pope himself, had acknowledged that his discussion of faith and good works had been constructive.

"What then should I be doing if I were now to retract these writings?" Luther asked. "Oh, wretched man! I alone, among all men living, should be abandoning truths approved by the unanimous voice of friends and enemies alike. I should be opposing doctrines that the whole world glories in confessing!"

Yes, he said brazenly, he had written against the Roman pope. Yes, he had attacked false doctrines, irregular and scandalous behavior that "afflicts the Christian world and ruins the souls of men." But he asked, "Is it not obvious that the laws and human doctrines of popes entangle, vex, and distress the consciences of the faithful?"

"No!" shouted out the emperor in horror.

Luther pressed on, unperturbed and undeterred. "No, your majesty, if I were to revoke what I have written on that subject, I should strengthen this tyranny and open an even wider door to many flagrant impieties." Turning his gaze directly on Charles V, he continued, "Not merely would the yoke that now weighs down Christians be made more grinding by my retraction . . . it would receive confirmation from your most serene majesty. Great God! I should thus be like an infamous cloak, used to hide and cover over every kind of malice and tyranny."

Turning then to the assemblage of princes, Luther gestured to Charles as "the young and noble prince, the Emperor Charles, on whom, next to God, we build so many hopes." Might his reign not be tormented by fatal abuses? He evoked the pharaohs and kings of Babylon who had been laid low by false measures. "God traps the crafty in their own snares!" And the Reformer spoke of God's justice. "'God moves mountains without their knowing it,'" he said, citing Job 9:5, "'and overturns them in his anger.'" Emperors take heed.

And yes, he had also written against the supporters of the Roman tyranny. Perhaps he had gone overboard in his invective against them, but they had set out to destroy faith. "I cannot sanction the impieties of my opponents," Luther proclaimed, "for they would crush God's people with still more cruelty."

For the papal representatives and the Catholic princes, his bombast was unbearable. But they could say nothing. The emperor had promised a fair hearing, had he not? The villain had his pulpit. How long would he go on? How far would he go?

Luther would make the most of it. In the ultimate arrogance and sacrilege in his detractors' eyes, he moved to associate himself with Christ himself, who had answered a high priest in the temple sharply and had been struck across the face by the guard standing by.

"I am not a saint," Luther said now. "As a mere man and not a god, I will defend myself after the example of Jesus Christ who said, 'If I have spoken evil, bear witness against me.'" Like Christ, he too was confronting the high priests and had been slapped for his sharp tongue. Now he challenged the emperor, the high prelates, and the illustrious lords to prove to him from Scripture where he was in error. If they could do so, he would be the first to commit his writings to the flames.

"And so," he said, turning back again to Charles V. "I commend myself to your august majesty, and your most serene highnesses. I beseech you in all humility not to permit the hatred of my enemies to rain upon me an indignation I have not deserved."

The inquisitor could stand it no longer. "You have not given any answer to the inquiry put to you!" he shouted. "You are not to question the decision of the councils. You are required to return a clear and distinct answer. Will you or will you not retract?"

Luther absorbed the blast calmly, undaunted: "Since your most serene majesty and your high mightinesses require of me a simple, clear, and direct answer, I will give one. I cannot submit my faith either to the pope or to the council, because it is clear as noonday that they have fallen into error and glaring inconsistency with themselves. If I am not convinced of any error by proof from Holy Scripture or by cogent reasons . . . and if my judgment is not in this way brought into subjugation to God's word, I neither can nor will retract anything. For it cannot be right for a Christian to speak against his country. God help me. Amen." (The widely quoted, famous phrase "Here I stand. I can say no more," which is often attributed to Luther at the end of his speech, is now largely discounted by modern historians.)

Pandemonium broke out. The emperor was confused. What had happened? He understood nothing of Luther's German. He commanded silence, and when it settled over the auditorium, he asked the witness to repeat his assertion in Latin.

"If you can't do it, Doctor, you've done enough!" a friendly voice shouted from the fringe.

Luther was again sweating profusely, but he repeated his discourse in Latin in flatter tones. Before his translation was finished, the emperor rose to his feet in fury and abruptly brought the proceedings to an end. "Take him away!" he ordered and left the hall swiftly by a side door. As Luther turned to leave, his supporters rushed to surround him. Spaniards fell in behind him, hissing and shouting out, "Into the fire, into the fire with him!" Luther turned on them with a gloat and raised his hands high in the air, in the manner of a victorious Teutonic swordsman. His followers did likewise, and out they strode.

But this show of bravado did not comport with Luther's true feelings of terror. Once outside and out of earshot, he whispered sullenly to a supporter.

"I am through. It's over."

Three

APPOINTMENT AT ALTENSTEIN

A s NIGHT FELL AFTER LUTHER'S BRAVURA PERFORMANCE AT the Imperial Diet, his adversaries huddled in various lairs in Worms. The ghost of Jan Huss had ascended from the lower depths, and the prelates were furious. But the clerics were divided about what to do. Some demanded that justice be done as it had been in the Council of Constance in 1415, when another "safe conduct" was scrapped, and Huss was hustled into the flames. Others gleaned from Luther's speech an openness to recant or at least to compromise.

When the proposal to scrap Luther's safe conduct was presented to Charles V, he recalled that the king of Bohemia of Huss's time, Sigismund, had come to live in history's disgrace for betraying his promise of indemnity to Huss. The young emperor also fretted about the possibility of a popular uprising if he were to proclaim an imperial ban against Luther, just as he, nearly a callow youth, was trying to assert his authority over all the German states.

Elector Frederick. By Albrecht Dürer. CREDIT: GEORGETOWN UNIVERSITY

Broadsheets were already circulating in the streets of Worms in which four hundred knights promised to defend Luther if he were threatened with capture. "A great wrong has been done!" the flyers announced. "We will fight with eight thousand men!" Such a threat could not be taken lightly.

The electors of Saxony met as well. Cardinal Aleander was informed that a majority favored an imperial ban. Even Luther's protector, the elector Frederick the Wise, seemed to be publicly wavering in his support. Of Luther's performance the day before, he said ruefully, "He was too daring for me." This was something of a pose for public consumption, since the elector was playing a double game.

For twenty-five years Frederick the Wise had been a quiet but stalwart advocate for reform, even though he still professed the Catholic faith. In 1505 he had established the university at Wittenberg to compete with his cousin's more established and distinguished institution at Leipzig. Frederick had been pleased with the notoriety Luther brought to his young institution. So taken was he with Luther's lectures on the Psalms that he pushed for their publication, and he had specifically raised Luther's salary to be sure that the firebrand would remain in Wittenberg.

Rome had done its best to persuade Frederick to arrest his professor after Luther's excommunication, even attempting to bribe him with the Golden Rose. (The blossom of pure gold was blessed by the pope on the fourth Sunday of Lent and given to the favored few as a token of reverent appreciation.) But despite the temptation, Frederick had refused.

Elector Frederick was also a great patron of the arts. Albrecht Dürer and Lucas Cranach, the elector's official court painter, were among his favored wards. It was said that his ducal castle contained some two thousand relics, including a thorn from Jesus's brow, straw from Christ's manger, four strands of the Virgin Mary's hair, a tear that Jesus shed at Lazarus's tomb, a piece of bread from the Last Supper, a twig from Moses's burning bush, and a drop of milk from the breast of the Virgin Mary herself.

Frederick was also keenly intelligent. The elector was known as "the Wise," but he was more cunning than wise. He shunned confrontation and was especially adverse to military action of any kind. This may have been because he controlled a lesser portion of Saxony while the greater parts were in the sway of his younger brother, John the Steady, and his cousin, Duke George (known as the Bearded, for his beard grew down to his waist). John smiled on reform, but he was less powerful than his older brother. Duke George was different. Deeply conservative and Luther's implacable enemy, he controlled Leipzig to the south, along with its fiercely Catholic university. If Luther was discovered in Duke George's dominion on his way home, he would be in grave danger.

If the majority of the delegates favored an imperial ban, they did so with various levels of enthusiasm. The young emperor listened to the arguments back and forth in silence.

At length, the emperor said, "*Eh bien*. I will tell you what I think."

At first Charles V spoke haltingly and with difficulty. His Hapsburg overbite slurred his words, and his adenoidal breathing caused breaks in his sentences. But what he said carried weight. He began with a discourse about the burden of his imperial ancestry that now stretched across the breadth of Europe and beyond to the New World, and he summoned a thousand years of Christian history to emphasize the enormity of the legacy it was now his duty to uphold. He was the scion of the Holy Roman emperors of Europe and Germany going back to Charlemagne; of the Catholic kings of Spain, Ferdinand and Isabella; of the margraves and archdukes of Austria dating back to the tenth century; of the Dukes of Burgundy stretching back to Charles the Bald and Philip the Bold. They were all, he proclaimed, true sons of the Roman church. They were defenders of the Catholic faith and its sacred customs and decrees. They all bequeathed to him this form of worship as his heritage.

"By their example I have lived," the emperor said. "I am determined to set my kingdoms and dominions, my friends, my body, my blood, my life, my soul upon that example. I hold fast to all that has happened since the Council of Constance," he avowed, referring to the fifteenth-century ecumenical council that had condemned and executed Jan Huss. "A single monk certainly errs if he sets himself against this grand precedent of all Christendom. Otherwise, Christendom itself would have erred for more than a thousand years."

"It would be a great shame to us and to you, members of the noble German Nation," Charles continued, "if in our time, through our negligence, we were to let even the appearance of heresy enter the hearts of men. You all heard Luther's speech yesterday. Now I say to you that I regret having delayed so long to act against him. I will not hear him again. He has my safe conduct for a few more days. But from now on I regard him as a notorious heretic and hope that all of you, as good Christians, will not be wanting in your duty."

Ironically, Luther's staunchest adversary, Duke George, spoke up. "What has been promised must be honored," he said gravely. "It would be an indelible stain on the rest of us if we were to break our word. Our ancestors would cover us with shame."

"Right and true, noble duke," the emperor responded. "If ever good faith is banished from the earth, she must take refuge in the court of princes."

In his imagination Luther would revisit this pivotal moment a number of times. Rather than gratitude to the emperor and the electors for deciding to maintain his safe conduct for a few more days, Luther conjured the scene with indignation. To a conclave of prelates many years later Luther remarked, "You did something to me there that is written with the point of a diamond, something that will never be erased until you are all dust blown with the wind. You sat there like masks and idols round that tender youth, the Emperor Charles, who was not versed in

Duke George of Saxony. Credit: Stiftung
Luthergedenkstätten in Sachsen-Anhalt, Wittenberg

such things and was bound to do your bidding. Uncomprehending, you condemned me unheard, and, as your consciences are my witness, wholly unjustly."

It was not true, however, that his case had not been heard at Worms, as Luther claimed. Indeed, on April 21, 1521, the matter of the emperor's response to Luther's provocations was still not completely settled. The emperor was troubled that night by the absolute nature of his decision and at the prospect that it would incite popular unrest. So he recruited the kindly and reasonable bishop of Trèves to gather a small, flexible group of prelates and nobles to make one last-minute effort to find some small ground for compromise that might avert a public disaster.

Some members of this hastily assembled conclave actually expressed admiration for much of Luther's work, stemming as it did from piety and good will. Could not the most controversial points of the infamous Ninety-Five Theses be put to some sort of local ecclesiastical adjudication? If Luther would recant a few of the more flagrantly offending points, perhaps he might even be appointed to a high priorate in Saxony. Perhaps the ban could be suspended or its execution postponed until a council could be impanelled at some point far in the future. Such a council could be German and not managed by the Roman Curia, a prospect Cardinal Aleander fiercely opposed.

When the proposition that he recant in exchange for leniency was put to him, Luther scoffed. "If this council be of men, it will come to naught," he said. "If it be of God, you cannot overturn it." *What exactly does he mean by that?* they wondered. A final resolution was left hanging.

Eventually, the bishop of Trèves gave up and delivered the last word.

"Since you have refused to listen to the advice of his majesty and the Orders of the empire, and confess your errors, it is now for the emperor to act. By his orders then, twenty days are allowed you to return to Wittenberg, free and under the protection of the prince's word, provided that on your journey you excite no disturbance by your conversation or preaching."

"Let it be done as the Lord wills," Luther replied. "Blessed be the name of God."

Luther's Safe Conduct document. CREDIT: DEUTSCHES HISTORISCHES MUSEUM, BERLIN

Later to a friend, the Reformer whispered, "If they did not spill my blood here, it's not because they lacked an inclination to murder, for homicide was in all their hearts." And indeed, many years later, Charles V would confirm what was in his heart. Regretting his high-mindedness as a moment of weakness, he remarked, "I did wrong in not killing Luther then and there. I was under no obligation to keep my word. I did not kill him, and, as a result, this mistake of mine assumed gigantic proportions. I could have prevented this."

ON APRIL 26, AFTER TEN DAYS IN THE MOUTH OF THE behemoth, Luther left Worms. Again in his rickety wagon, he was accompanied by his friend and fellow theologian from

Wittenberg, Nicholas von Amsdorf, and a simple friar named Johannes Petzensteiner.

Beyond the gates of Worms an escort of mounted guards joined the wagon, and not long afterward the imperial herald—a rough customer named Kaspar Sturm—turned up. If Luther seemed remarkably cavalier in the face of his peril, it was because he knew there was a clandestine plan afoot. Through intermediaries Frederick the Wise had informed him the night before his departure that he would be guided to a place of safety and that he was not to worry. The elector himself was kept in the dark about the operation's details, including the actual place where Luther was to be taken. He wanted to be able to deny any knowledge, should the emperor or the Diet suspect him of collusion.

North of Oppenheim the little wagon and its escort crossed over the Rhine River, spent a night in Frankfurt, and moved farther north along the languid Fulda River. At the tiny village of Friedberg, Luther tarried for several days to write a long letter to the emperor. He may have known that Charles was moving on to more pressing matters. But Luther was writing for posterity now, and the letter was intended more for his printer than for his sovereign.

The Reformer was intent on creating his own historical record. Repeating his willingness to appear before ecclesiastical and lay judges who were above suspicion, who were scholarly and open-minded, he wrote to Charles that he would accept instruction, "provided there was recourse to the manifest, clear, free Word of God." The proviso was the sticking point.

If these opaque, comfortable words were written for history, Luther's true state of mind was evident in a letter he wrote at the same time to Lucas Cranach, with whom he was soon to collaborate on his masterwork. "My view was that His Imperial Majesty should have assembled doctors, one or fifty of them, and honestly vanquished me," Luther told his friend. "But instead all that happened was: Are the books yours?—Yes—Are you willing to retract them?—No—Then go. Oh, we blind Germans! How childishly we behave, and how we let ourselves be so abominably mocked and duped by the Roman scholars." He informed Cranach that for a time he would "shut up." But then, shutting up had never been easy for him.

Handing the letters to his imperial herald, Luther instructed Sturm to deliver the one for the emperor and post the letter to Cranach. The herald's protective services were no longer needed, he announced. Without imperial protection, vulnerable now to any dutiful Catholic hero who truly reviled all heresy, he continued on his journey. Only Nicholas von Amsdorf and the nervous little monk Petzensteiner accompanied him now.

North of Fulda they arrived at the ancient Benedictine monastery, which dated back to the year 742. There Luther was welcomed by the abbot, who fed him sumptuously, lent his bed to his guest, and then, the next morning, implored him to preach in his monastery. At first, Luther demurred, knowing full well that such sermonizing would break the promise of silence on which his safe conduct depended, and fearing that the monastery might lose its royal privileges as a result. But the temptation was too great, and he soon relented. Why not? "After all," he said. "it's more important to obey God than men."

Luther's stay had a great impact: after he departed, the abbot allowed his monks to abandon their vows and leave the monastery.

Farther east, Luther was bolder still. Ascending to the pulpit of a local church, he preached with gusto, even though a Catholic curate, a notary, and two official witnesses sat scowling in the audience to document Luther's insubordination.

THE AMBUSH CAME A DAY LATER.

Eight days into his journey home, on a side road near Altenstein Castle, two masked horsemen burst from behind a large beech tree and fell upon the little wagon. Friar Petzensteiner leapt to the ground and scampered into the woods, while Luther hid in the back of the wagon. With bow drawn, one of the horsemen demanded to know if one Martin Luther was present in the wagon. The monk emerged, appearing fearful like an apprehended criminal. Amid shouts and curses and rough handling—all for the benefit of anyone who might be watching in the bushes—the masked men hustled Luther along to a waiting horse, while von Amsdorf watched the farce with secret bemusement. Down the road Luther was given a false beard to wear. For the next six hours the little band crisscrossed the back roads of the Thuringian forest to confuse any possible pursuers.

Within a few hours, the imposing Wartburg Castle loomed in the distance.

Wartburg Castle. CREDIT: WARTBURG FOUNDATION.

Four

PATMOS

TOWARD MIDNIGHT ON MAY 6, 1521, THE DRAWBRIDGE OF the Wartburg was lowered, and the castle's stern captain, Hans von Berlepsch, received a tired and bedraggled Luther unceremoniously. At first, the captain was kept in the dark about the true identity of his mysterious guest, but the commander had his instructions. Luther was escorted to two small rooms high atop the castle. They could only be reached with a long ladder, which was to be removed at night. The two small windows in the parapet were glazed with opaque bull's-eye panes, and thus the resident was deprived of a view across the lovely sylvan foothills of the Thuringian forest. The furnishings of his quarters were spare: a desk, an inkwell, a wooden pallet, and a straight-backed chair.

Luther was ordered to discard his monk's cowl, to dress in knight's garb, and to let his hair and beard grow. He was to be known forthwith as Junker Jörg (Knight George), as if he were a knight errant of a minor noble house who was friendly with high personages and was being hidden after some unspecified political difficulty.

He settled in for a long stay—as long, Luther imagined, as
Leo X, the Florentine pontiff who had condemned him, should
live.

The peril of Luther's presence in the Wartburg had been emphasized to his assiduous and attentive jailer. The knight was to
be kept incommunicado, while at the same time he was to be
treated courteously and kept well supplied with the comforts of
home, including plenty of game and his favorite Rhenish wine.
Within a few days the restrictions were relaxed, and a procedure
was worked out whereby Luther could send and receive letters
from certain persons in safe places within the domain of Elector
Frederick. In the coming months the hostage would take full advantage of this privilege.

His correspondents were principally three. The first and most
important was Philipp Melanchthon. He was a brilliant young
Greek scholar who hailed from southern Germany and whose
real name was Schwarzerde, or "Black Earth." But since he had
demonstrated extraordinary proficiency in Greek as a youth, his
father had changed his last name to its Greek translation. In his
teenage years he had sat at the feet of the great humanist of the
age, Erasmus of Rotterdam. At the age of eighteen he had been
appointed a professor of Greek at Wittenberg.

Soon after his installation, he and Luther had bonded.
Though seventeen years separated their ages, they formed a lifelong friendship. To some they must have appeared to be an odd
couple. On Luther's part, the bond was paternal. Melanchthon
was thin and wiry, slight of stature, and Luther would come to
call him his "little Greek." Though Melanchthon admired and
revered his first mentor, Erasmus, with whom Luther would develop profound differences, he was even more enamored of Luther and embraced his theological stance.

Comparing himself to Melanchthon, Luther would write, "I
am rough, boisterous, stormy, and altogether war-like. I am born

to fight against monsters and Devils. I must remove stumps and stones, cut away thistles and thorns and clear wild forests. But Master Philipp comes along softly, gently sowing and watering with joy, according to the gifts which God has abundantly bestowed upon him." With his skills of communication and empathy, Melanchthon would later come to be known as "the diplomat of the Reformation." People with troubles were drawn to him for comfort, so much so that Luther invented a new word for him, *sorgenblutegel*, meaning a leech that takes the sorrows of others into his blood.

Luther's power over his disciple was considerable. A year after his arrival in Wittenberg, for example, Luther insisted that Melanchthon marry the daughter of the town's mayor, much to Melanchthon's sorrow. He would call his wedding day "the day of my greatest misery." Gradually the scholar established himself as a popular lecturer in the ancient languages and the classics. He was an educator, not a priest, and as a layman was by instinct a diplomat who recoiled from confrontation. Precise in his thinking to the point of obsession, he possessed the great skill of reducing complicated theological arguments to simple propositions and clear, accessible prose. This would prove to be an invaluable talent in the months and years ahead. Now, in Luther's absence, it fell to Melanchthon to safeguard the theological purity of their fledgling movement.

The second correspondent was the elector's intimate adviser George Spalatin. A priest who had received his degree from Wittenberg, he was now the electoral court's librarian and chaplain. Luther could be sure that any communication he had with Spalatin would be shared with Frederick the Wise.

And then there was Luther's third correspondent: Nicholas von Amsdorf, the Wittenberg professor who had been Luther's companion along the rough road to and from Worms. After witnessing Luther's staged abduction, Amsdorf had returned to

Philipp Melanchthon by Albrecht Dürer.
CREDIT: GEORGETOWN UNIVERSITY

Wittenberg University, and now he, like Melanchthon, could keep the Reformer apprised of developments in his hometown.

On May 8, only two days after he was settled in his fortress, Luther penned his first letters to Melanchthon. In the first he emphasized the necessity of secrecy about his whereabouts, for "who knows what these mighty men have planned. It is not necessary that people besides yourself know anything other than that I am still alive." He evoked a line from Psalms 4:4: "Commune with your own heart upon your bed, and be still." In the second letter, he wrote about students at Erfurt University rioting against the Catholic authorities responsible for excommunicating the priests who had welcomed him on the way to Worms. Naturally, he feared that the disruption would be laid at the door of his brittle movement. "I'm amazed that this is tolerated," Luther groused. "Although it's good that these lazy, ungodly priests are harassed,

yet this creates disgrace and justified repulsion for our gospel. . . .
It will be said that we are not yet worthy before God to be servants of his Word. Satan mocks and ridicules our efforts."

If Reformers did not act in accordance with their gospel, their
movement would wither like the fig tree in the Bible, he wrote,
invoking Matthew 21:19, in which Jesus orders a fig tree to bear
no fruit, and it immediately withers. Luther feared that after the
disruptions of its rowdy students, Erfurt University might become "a second Prague," a reference to the precipitous decline of
Prague University after its students rioted in support of the heretic Jan Huss more than a hundred years before.

R UMORS WERE FLYING AROUND EUROPE ABOUT LUTHER'S
whereabouts. Some in Wittenberg believed that the Reformer was dead, poisoned by his worst enemies. Much more important than the Wittenberg gossip was the attitude of his most
dangerous enemies. Far away on the banks of the Rhine, Cardinal
Aleander was convinced that friendly parties had kidnapped the
outlaw and were sequestering him to the south, in Franconia. It
was probable, the cardinal thought, that a noble named Sylvester
von Schaumberg had made good on his standing offer of military
protection.

But Cardinal Aleander had a more immediate, tangible challenge. He had set to work on drafting the Edict of Worms, the
official decree that would codify the decision of Charles V and
his council about how to deal with the recalcitrant monk. At
last, his long road was coming to a most satisfactory end. Embrac-
ing his assignment with joy and satisfaction, he adopted a direct,
unembellished style he felt would appeal to the straightforward
German mind. Luther was a "Devil" who had assumed the likeness of a monk, the successor to the heretic Jan Huss: "He has
sullied marriage, disparaged confession, and denied the body and

blood of our Lord. He makes the sacraments depend on the faith of the recipient. He is pagan in his denial of free will. This Devil in monk's clothes has brought together all the ancient errors in one stinking puddle and has invented new ones."

And then with relish the cardinal penned his damnation: "Luther is to be regarded as a convicted heretic." Now that Luther's safe conduct had expired, "no one is to harbor him. His followers also are to be condemned. His books are to be eradicated from the memory of man." No one was to provide food or shelter to the villain. The penalties for disobeying the Edict of Worms were severe: loss of benefits and liberties to any prince or town that contravened the Edict. No one was to "compose, write, print, sell, buy, or secretly or openly keep" any of Luther's works. If the outlaw was apprehended, he was to be handed over swiftly to the Inquisition. To the pious hero who accomplished this sacred duty, a handsome reward was offered.

Several weeks later, on May 25, 1521, at a High Mass at Worms, Charles V signed the document with a flourish. When the Mass was ended, the emperor turned to Cardinal Aleander and said, "You will be content now."

"Yes," the nuncio replied. "And even greater will be the contentment of His Holiness and of all Christendom."

Shortly afterward, the emperor slipped away, boarding a barge going south down the Rhine River toward Italy, where a more immediate crisis awaited him. Four days after Luther's defense at Worms, France had declared war on Charles and his dominions in Italy, and the imperial focus shifted to the disputed city of Milan and rebellious communities in Spain. A four-year war in Italy was about to begin. The pope in Rome would be forced to choose between Charles V and Francis I of France. Suddenly, the matter of a satanic monk in faraway Germany receded in importance, at least for a time.

Frederick the Wise had departed days before Charles, fleeing not only the unpleasant conclave but also the noxious vapors of Worms, for plague was abroad in its cobblestone streets. The elector did not want to be party to the debate over Luther's fate, much less sanction the final language of the condemnation. Moreover, he did not want to be questioned further about Luther's whereabouts. He could honestly profess ignorance about where his protégé was hiding, if indeed the fugitive was still alive.

With a straight face he avowed his unqualified support of the Vatican, but his real attitude toward the whole proceeding at Worms was reflected in a letter he sent to his brother, John the Steady. At Worms, he wrote, Luther had for enemies Ananias and Caiaphas, Herod and Pilate—in other words, sanctimonious high priests, fierce antagonists, royal murderers, and cowardly judges.

A T FIRST, LUTHER SEEMED TO BE ENJOYING THE RUMORS OF his demise. His enemies were chanting, "When will he die and his name perish?" he wrote to Melanchthon in the May 12 letter. He gave his most prominent adversaries unflattering monikers from the Old Testament. Duke George, his bête noire, had become the "Rehoboam of Dresden" after the deeply ambitious but spiritually empty king of Judah in 1 Kings 11:43ff (though sometimes Luther shortened this to "the Hog of Dresden"). Another bitter foe, Joachim I of Brandenburg, was dubbed the "Ben-hadad of Damascus" (1 Kings: 20:5ff) after the king of Syria known for his arrogance in prosperity and his cowardice in adversity. "The Lord will laugh at them," Luther chortled, for the kings of the earth had set themselves against the Lord.

Still, Luther felt it necessary to buck up the courage of his disciple. "Be steadfast," he wrote to Melanchthon, "for you are now the minister of the Word. Fortify the walls and towers of Jerusalem, for the enemy will soon attack you as well. We carry this burden together. At this point I stand alone in the battle. Soon they come after you." Melanchthon was Elisha to his Elijah (2 Kings 2:9).

And yet the monk's letters in the first month of his captivity reflected his worry about what would happen to his fragile movement in his absence. Who would preach in his stead at the parish church of Wittenberg (*Stadtpfarrkirche*)? And what might they say? He craved gossip. "Is Amsdorf still snoring and lazy?" he asked Melanchthon. "What is Doctor Karlstadt doing?" he wondered, as if he deduced already who presented the greatest, internal danger in the coming months. He vented frustration. "I am annoyed that not a single copy of your *Loci* has arrived here," he complained, referring to Melanchthon's masterwork, the first systematic exposition of Reformation doctrine. Its printing had begun in April but would not be finished until December. Amid this mixture of turbulent emotions, Luther exuded grandiosity: "Though I should perish, the gospel will lose nothing."

But most of all it was Melanchthon's grit that concerned him. At some point in their correspondence, the disciple had complained that, in Luther's absence, he and his fellow Reformers were losing their sense of direction and unity.

In response Luther invoked the passage in Matthew about sheep without a shepherd (9:36) and wrote to his friend, "I cannot believe what you write, that you are going astray without a shepherd. This would be the saddest and bitterest news. As long as you, Amsdorf, and the others are there, you are not without a shepherd. Don't talk that way lest God be angered, and we be found guilty of ingratitude. Would that all the churches had one-fourth of your share of the Word and one-fourth of its ministers!"

He signed his May 12 letter as Martin Luther, "in the land of the birds."

During his first weeks at the Wartburg, after the din and strife of Worms, and after the combat of the past four years since his

Ninety-Five Theses, he lapsed into an unsettled, dreamlike state, at once luxuriating in silence and lassitude. "Here I am drunk with leisure, like a free man among captives," he wrote. At the same time he was suffering with chronic stomach pain. Though he was beset by these competing physical and psychological afflictions, his idleness would not last.

On May 15 Luther's safe conduct expired. He was now an official outlaw. Ten days later, on the last day of the Diet of Worms, before a virtually empty assembly, the Edict of Worms was formally issued. It read: "We forbid anyone from this time forward to dare, either by words or by deeds, to receive, defend, sustain, or favor the said Martin Luther. On the contrary, we want him to be apprehended and punished as a notorious heretic, as he deserves, to be brought personally before us, or to be securely guarded until those who have captured him inform us. Whereupon, we will order the appropriate manner of proceeding against the said Luther." The "appropriate" manner surely referred to the Inquisition's incineration of the apostates Jan Huss and Girolamo Savonarola. The Edict ended with the promise of a reward for anyone who aided in the heretic's capture.

Luther had anticipated its harshness. "They will now search the whole world for my little books," he wrote to Melanchthon, "and in so doing swiftly prepare their own destruction." To another supporter he wrote of being a strange prisoner at the Wartburg, "since I sit here both willingly and unwillingly: willingly since the Lord wants it this way; unwillingly, since I would want to stand up in public for the Word of God, but I have not yet been worthy of this."

IN MAY, AS LUTHER STRUGGLED TO COME TO GRIPS WITH HIS isolation, the first Catholic priests began divesting themselves of their celibacy vows and marrying. Among them was a former student of Luther's and also a pastor at Hersfeld who had been transfixed by Luther's provocative sermon there a few weeks earlier in violation of his safe conduct. In the coming months a number of others would follow suit. It was as if the dam had burst. Of this rush to cast aside vows and marry, Luther would say later, "In their haste to marry, it is carnal impulses that those monks were obeying."

By the end of May, restless and determined not to be laid low by his physical suffering, Luther grew tired of his leisure and settled down to work. He had arrived at the Wartburg with only two possessions, both of which he had hidden beneath his friar's cloak: a New Testament in Greek and an Old Testament in Hebrew. At the castle he had no access to a library on whose works he might rely for his new theological writings. What research materials he might require Philipp Melanchthon would have to send to him from Wittenberg, and this would prove to be a scattershot proposition.

At first through May and June 1521 his kinetic energy seemed to swing wildly between different plans and projects. On May 26 he wrote to Melanchthon about the necessity of answering another sharp attack from organized opposition at the University of Louvain. Theologians there and at the University of Cologne had allied themselves in their condemnation of Luther. This was no academic exercise, for the two Universities combined in their attacks and sent their findings to the grand inquisitor in Spain. He was Cardinal Adriaan Florensz, a bloodless Dutchman who was then the bishop of Tortosa and the viceroy to Emperor Charles V—and most importantly, the next pope after Leo X.

Luther was uncowed by the academics' rejection. Titling his response, *Against the Asses of Louvain and Cologne*, he complained that the supercilious professors of the universities had condemned his works without basis and compared their tracts to the betrayals of Herod and Pilate.

In the coming months his main focus, he announced, would be to translate his commentaries on the Epistles and Gospels into German. It was imperative, he felt, that the common person understand the great themes of Christianity. Since only about 5 percent of the German population was literate, this was a problem. At the time, the better part of church ritual was still presented publicly in Latin. This instinct—to translate his doctrine into the tongue of the people—would prove to be the seed of the greatest work Luther would produce at the Wartburg, and it continued a pattern that began four years earlier. In 1518 Luther had published a tract explaining the Ten Commandments, the Lord's Prayer, and the Nicene Creed in simple, vernacular German. Now he wanted to focus on Advent and Christmas. But to do that he needed to receive his past notes on these subjects that had been written and published in Latin. By June 10 he still had not received his Latin Advent homilies from Melanchthon and, in annoyance, had to change his plans.

Another past work Luther completed and expanded in this first month in captivity was his treatise on confession, a subject with great political as well as religious significance. He had addressed this Catholic sacrament before Worms, because he had learned to his disgust that Catholic priests were using the confessional booth to glean whether certain penitents were secretly reading Luther's banned books. In his treatise now he instructed his supporters on how to answer such inappropriate spying by inquisitive confessors. He told them to say: "Please, Father, do not chase me into a corner and put me in difficulty. I have come to confession for you to absolve me of my sins, not to cause me distress." And should the snooping priest not relent, they should continue by saying: "Please, sir, you are a Father Confessor, not a task master. It is my duty to confess what is on my conscience. It is not your duty to press me, nor to probe my private affairs.

You might as well be asking me how much money I have in my pocket." It was the priest's obligation, in turn, to grant absolution, and then if he chose, "argue the matter out with Luther or the pope." The confessing person should then tell the prying priest, "Do not make the sacrament of confession into a danger for me." And should the confessor refuse absolution on this basis, wrote Luther, the penitent should regard him as an imposter and a thief, guilty of withholding what was the penitent's right.

Do not be alarmed, the Reformer summed up in his treatise. Know that by the mere act of confession the penitent has received absolution in God's sight. No intermediary, not even the pope, had the right to demand a person's confession, nor to deny absolution.

Luther dedicated his treatise to one of his most important and militant supporters, Franz von Sickingen. Von Sickingen was a powerful leader of the Estate of Knights, a coalition of free knights. These renegades presided over independent fiefdoms and commanded private armies, and they opposed the influence of Rome. In Luther's rebellion they perceived a useful tool to undercut the power of the church and advance their independence and power. Ironically, von Sickingen had been an early supporter of Charles V in his bid to be elected Holy Roman emperor. But when Luther came to Worms, the knight had offered him the protection of his nearby castle. If von Sickingen was exploiting Luther and his movement for his own political gain, Luther was no less exploiting the knight and his powerful private army for his physical protection. The Reformer needed all the help he could get to discourage Rome and the emperor from tracking him down in his hideout and enforcing the Edict of Worms.

On June 1 Luther sent his treatise on confession to von Sickingen along with a fascinating letter. In it the Reformer referred to his situation at the Wartburg for the first time as his Patmos, a reference to the remote Greek island where, it was said, John the Evangelist wrote the Book of Revelation. Now he was sending his own "revelation" to von Sickingen to show his gratitude for the knight's succor.

"I have been pushed off the field," Luther wrote. His adversaries had a little time now to change their behavior, and if they did not change it, "someone else will change their ways for them. . . . Thanks be to God that there is now less fear and dread of the bugaboo at Rome. The world can now break its spell."

As Luther entered his third month in his "Patmos," he continued to fret, with good reason, about what was happening in Wittenberg. He began to doubt that Melanchthon, with his gentle ways, was capable of holding the movement together. Rome was surely marshaling its forces and preparing to crush the rebellion without mercy. The full weight of that power would fall on his supporters, and they would have to bear the onslaught without him. "I cannot be free of worry that wolves may enter the sheepfold now that I am away," he wrote. By "wolves" he meant "Roman tyrants," but there were other poltroons within the flock itself to concern him.

"Since not all of you are of equally stout heart," he wrote to Melanchthon, no doubt implicating his disciple in that shortcoming, he wished to send along a little comfort to the poor people of Wittenberg who might need bucking up. Indeed, following his missive to Melanchthon, he wrote an extraordinary letter to the home team. Its bravado can stand in all of literature as one of the most powerful exhortations for a hard-pressed, vulnerable cadre of rebels.

Characteristically, the letter to the stalwarts began with Scripture. He attached a commentary on Psalm 37: he said the psalm perfectly fit their needs, "since in an especially loving and motherly way it quiets rising anger against the arrogant slanderers. . . . Of course, the evildoers will be puffed up for some time until they are deflated." Psalm 37 said it better: "Fret not thyself because of evildoers, neither be thou envious against the workers of iniquity. For they shall soon be cut down like the grass, and wither as the green herb" (37:1–2).

In the past few months he had conflated his situation at Worms with Christ's entrance to Jerusalem. At the Wartburg he saw himself as John the Evangelist at Patmos. Now he presented himself to the people of Wittenberg as the incarnation of St. Paul during the apostle's imprisonment at Rome (Acts 21–22), even though unlike St. Paul, Luther could not comfort his converted merely out of the riches of his own spirit. As the "blood thirsty murderers of souls" threatened his flock, they should remember that they possessed the "true and pure gospel" that had been revealed to them by God through "poor me."

Their enemies preferred to avoid the light of open engagement: "They howl 'Hoo-hoo' in the dark like owls and think they can frighten us with this!" He ridiculed the papal legate at Worms and the professors and priests at previous contests like Augsburg in 1518 and Leipzig in 1519, calling them braggarts who thought they were smarter than everyone else. "I let them bleed themselves to death and slander to the point of exhaustion." They put on a big show with their vicious writings, he wrote. They hoped to cover up or dress up their disgrace from the common person. But their authors were as talented for the job as "the ass is talented for playing the harp!"

Meanwhile, the furious pace of his work continued. There was much unfinished work to be completed. The year before he had received a plaintive, heartfelt letter from a seventeen-year-old prince, John Frederick of Saxony, who was the landgrave of Thuringia, a student of his colleague Spalatin at Wittenberg, and the nephew of Frederick the Wise. In it the young prince wrote of his terror over Leo X's excommunication bull and was asking for reassurance. The letter moved Luther for its faith and youthful searching. But it also filled the Reformer with sympathy for a young man who was soon to assume great responsibilities of power. (John Frederick would become a lifelong supporter of the Reformation, even though Emperor Charles V would imprison him for his support of Luther and threaten him with execution.)

Luther had begun writing his answer to young John Frederick during the past winter, but the Diet of Worms interrupted the task. Now, high above the Thuringian forest, he returned to the challenge. His reply would take the form of an exposition of the Magnificat, or Mary's Canticle, whose text came from Luke 1:42–55 and concerned the visitation of the Blessed Mary to her cousin Elizabeth, who was then pregnant. (The child in her womb was John, later John the Baptist.) At seeing Mary, Elizabeth cries out: "Blessed art thou among women, and blessed is the fruit of thy womb." And Mary replies with her canticle, a moving expression of her deep faith, often sung in Christian churches in evening prayer, especially Lutheran vespers: "My soul doth magnify the Lord. . . ."

Luther finished his missive to John Frederick in June. Entitled "Magnificat," his portrait of Mary is that of a tender mother and an ordinary woman, coming from a "low estate and nothingness," the issue of "poor, despised and lowly parents," whose soul is guided by the Holy Ghost and whose heart leaps for joy in praising God. Some have suggested that Luther was inspired by the images of Mary painted by his famous admirer Albrecht Dürer. Early in the century, Dürer had produced a series of prints called *Marienleben* in his distinctive style. The style of Luther's "Magnificat" is equally admired, and thought to prefigure his great work of translation to come.

During these productive days, Luther also finished his treatise on confession with its preamble to Frederick von Sickingen and sent it off for printing. He was thinking about translating the prayers of Psalm 119 on the obedience to divine law, for the Psalms generally would be a lifelong obsession. Of them, he would write, "The Holy Scriptures are to believing souls what the meadow is to the animal, what home is to man, the nest to the birds, the cleft of the rock to sea fowl, the stream to the fish." While he still waited for Melanchthon to send his previous work on Advent, he had completed a homily for Christmas Eve. He was scribbling without interruption. As if his writings were not prodigious enough, he was also studying Hebrew and Greek.

But far away and in high places, his opposition was mobilizing.

Five

LOWLY MONK VERSUS LOFTY KING

T HE ESTIMABLE KING OF ENGLAND, HENRY VIII, WAS EAGER to contain the virus of Luther's movement, for he was genuinely shocked at the reports he had received from the Diet of Worms. The king's ambassador at the Imperial Diet had sent back regular reports on the horrifying proceedings against the heretic. Conveying one of the tracts to Cardinal Thomas Wolsey, the king's top advisor, the envoy wrote, "Burn it when ye have done with it," as if the reptilian ideas contained in the document might escape and multiply on English soil.

As the Diet raced toward its dramatic conclusion with Luther's extraordinary performance, the same envoy urged Wolsey to gather all the printers and booksellers of England and command them not to bring any more of Luther's books into the country nor to permit further translation, "lest there ensue great trouble to the realm and to the Church of England." Wolsey responded by ordering all existing copies of the blasphemous material to be delivered to the local bishopric. This was a tall order, for Luther's works had been filtering into England for four years. Wolsey's injunction could scarcely sweep them all up.

Cardinal Wolsey was then the most powerful man in England after the king. Holding the posts of royal almoner, registrar of the Order of the Garter, archbishop of York, and Lord Chancellor, Wolsey had promised reforms to the English church but had never delivered. Surrounding himself with pomp and luxury, he instead dedicated himself to one proposition: to advance the reputation of his king and make Henry VIII the arbiter of European politics. To Shakespeare the Lord Chancellor was a fox, equally as ravenous as he was subtle and "as prone to mischief as able to perform it." The son of a butcher, he was also immensely fat. Shakespeare had described him as a "keech" or congealed lump of fat whose bulk "takes up the rays of the beneficial sun and keeps them from the earth." He was also brilliant and cunning. And he had sired two children by his mistress, Joan Larke, with whom he had lived openly for ten years.

On May 12, 1521, only six days after Luther arrived at the Wartburg, Cardinal Wolsey traveled to St. Paul's Cathedral in central London with great fanfare. At the altar, surrounded by the grandees of the English Catholic church, including the archbishop of Canterbury, he knelt to pray. Then, arranging his massive girth upon a throne, a cross in either hand, he listened as John Fisher, the bishop of Rochester, condemned Luther and all his works. As the bishop spoke, Luther's most notorious book, *The Babylonian Captivity of the Church*, and others of his works were placed on a pile of wood. When the fire was lit, the crowd shouted, "Long live the pope! Long live the king!"

Across England a lame anti-Luther campaign was undertaken to stem the tide of contagion. One tract in the effort was titled "A Little Handkerchief for Luther's Spittle." But the Reformer had his English boosters, both public and secret. At Oxford University several popular lecturers spread the new theology, and students embraced it eagerly. Cambridge University was similarly infected. High officials in the English church vainly tried to resist the virus's spread. "What a pity it is," wrote the archbishop of Kent, "that through the lewdness of one or two cankered members of the faculty who are seducing the young, a whole university should run into infamy of so heinous a crime." Still, the archbishop thought the less said, the better.

France, like England, wrestled with how to deal with the scourge. On April 15, 1521, the faculty of theology at the Sorbonne published its condemnation of Luther. For more than a year, French theologians had been divided about Luther's propositions. Some admired the vigor of his expression and deplored the practice of indulgences, while the conservative majority, eager to protect the Sorbonne's reputation for impeccable orthodoxy in doctrinal matters, pushed to denounce Luther's radical doctrines. Rome's excommunication together with the Edict of Worms settled the matter.

Finally, the Parisian theologians arrived at a consensus, and a damning verdict called "The Determination of the Parisian Faculty upon Luther" was published. It identified and condemned 113 of Luther's propositions. Specifically, the professors denounced these axioms: that the sacraments were of recent invention; that all Christians were priests and empowered to preach the gospel; that the Mass is not a sacrifice; that neither a pope nor a bishop had the right to establish obligations or rules for the believer; that monastic vows should be abolished; that a confessional contrition encourages hypocrisy; and that the soul does not cease sinning in purgatory.

As Luther had settled into the Wartburg, the French campaign to eradicate his ideas began. It became a criminal offense to publish or sell Luther's books without a faculty stamp of approval.

With fanfare the king of France issued a decree that all Luther's books be handed in to Parliament within a week. With Gallic drollery Francis I proclaimed Luther to be a "sad person."

From the Wartburg Luther responded to the eminences of the Sorbonne with scorn, proclaiming them to be "theologasters," or religious phonies full of hot air. Instead of dignifying their arguments against him, he composed a satirical dialogue that ridiculed the French professors as clowns with beards as long as their black costumes. The satirical dialogue has three characters, a self-important doctor called Eck (the name of his prosecutor at Worms), a barber, and a confessor.

"Good morrow, Master Eck," the confessor begins.

"Good morrow, father."

"Why do you send for me?"

"To confess."

"Begin," says the confessor.

"I am a master of arts, master in theology, doctor, chancellor ordinary, doctor in canon law, doctor in civil law. . . . "

"Your sins, doctor, not your titles."

"My sins?" the doctor echoes.

"Yes, drunkenness?"

"I am always thirsty."

"Lechery?"

"You mean frailty of the flesh?"

"Envy?"

"The favorite sin of the clergy."

"Anger?"

"Who can subdue his passions?"

Frustrated at these non-answers, the confessor cries, "Why then did you send for me?"

The doctor then confesses all the sins that prompted him to condemn Luther's works. He is offered absolution but refuses, since given free will, he cannot absolve himself of all his sins. And so the confessor has him tied down and instructs the barber to shave his head.

"My God!" exclaims the astonished confessor. "What is this? Lice?"

"No," cries the doctor. "Syllogisms, propositions, majors, minors, corollaries, and the whole artillery of the schoolman."

Luther's spoof ends with a long paragraph of self-congratulation.

"Luther is not a saint, yet you deem him to be a god," a courtier remarks. "What has he done to be so adored?"

"What has he done?" a burgher responds. "He has taught us to keep our money in our pockets, and not spend it in the purchase of indulgences. What has he done? He has taught us that a layman has as much power as a monk and a priest. What has he done? He has taught us to laugh at Aristotle. What has he done? He has taught us that the pope is a miserable sinner. What has he done? He has taught us that there is only one book we ought to read: the Bible. What has he done? He has taught us that all courtiers are blackguards."

To support his great mentor, Philipp Melanchthon followed with a more sober rebuttal to the Parisian theologians. In 1521 in a pamphlet entitled *Against the Furious Decree of the Parisian Theologasters*, Melanchthon wrote, "It will be easier for you to find Christ among the carpenters than among these people."

Just as the thin, intense Martin Luther of the Wartburg bore no relation to the subsequent pudgy figure of popular imagination, so Henry VIII at this time did not resemble the stout, pasty image of his advancing years. Eight years younger than Luther, Henry had been monarch for twelve years and was only thirty years old in 1521. In both of them the vibrancy of passion and ambition burned at its brightest. Henry was, as one wry historian would put it, still in Act 1 of his life. (Act 2, his later life, was defined as a period when "he spared neither men in his hate nor women in his lust.") Now he was tall and broad-shouldered, athletic, learned, and clever, accomplished in languages, disquisition, and music. Still devoted to his queen, Catherine of Aragon, his frustration with her was just beginning, for five years earlier she had borne him his only surviving child, Mary (later known as Bloody Mary). He could hope that Catherine might still produce a son. It would be another four years before he became infatuated with the court flirt, Anne Boleyn. And notably, he was still a faithful son of the Catholic Church.

By education and temperament, the king was deeply interested in theology, but he also appreciated its political utility. In the Luther crisis he saw an opportunity not only to exercise his considerable intelligence and display his theological rectitude, but also to ingratiate himself further with Pope Leo X and, perhaps most significantly, to advance his standing vis-á-vis the other powerful monarchs of Europe. The king of England bridled at his status as something of a second-class monarch. The Holy Roman emperor, Charles V, presided over a vast domain across Europe that stretched from Spain to Denmark, the Netherlands to Austria. Francis I, in turn, reigned over the richest land on the continent. In the global politics of Europe, the small island kingdom of England was often considered an afterthought. Moreover, Leo X had honored both Charles V and Francis I with the designation of "defender of the faith." It was a distinction Henry VIII desperately coveted as well. Was he any lesser a king or less a defender of the true faith than they?

Indubitably, the English king was at this point genuinely and viscerally affronted by Luther's assault on the Roman church. The Reformer had become a revolutionary; his writings had moved from pondering the fine points of theology to provocative religious agitation and political rebellion. The masses had begun to question the foundation of both religious and secular authority. Bold and reckless, his eloquence was stirring national aspirations in Germany and other countries in Europe. "I am at a loss to know whether the pope be the anti-Christ or merely his apostle," Luther had written to George Spalatin two years earlier. Such slurs offended Henry deeply.

It was not only that this rogue was working to undermine the primacy of the pope, to disparage the necessity for good works, to destroy the time-honored practice of indulgences, to deny the seven sacraments, and to denigrate the saints. Not only that. Infuriatingly, the villain was pursuing these horrors in a contemptuous, impertinent, and indeed joyful manner. Luther's ridicule and irony were proving to be his most effective and most grating weapons. When his opponents invoked the logic of Aristotle, for example, he compared that method of reasoning to the ass that Patriarch Abraham left behind when he went up the mountain to make his sacrifice. And the Reformer seemed utterly oblivious to the danger he faced in his rebellion. Indeed, he seemed to embrace martyrdom. Of the pope's warnings about personal consequences, Luther had replied, "What will be the most he can do? Deprive me of two or three days' existence? My hours are numbered. Let us sing a hymn of thanksgiving to the Lord."

If Henry was to seize the reins of a countermovement, what should he attack? His juiciest targets were the three widely disseminated, confrontational treatises Luther had penned in the previous year. The first was called *To the Christian Nobility of the German Nation*. If one overlooked its most outrageous taunts—and there were many—it was a legitimate call to ecclesiastical reform. To be sure, it denigrated the pope and "the Roman Sodom." It deplored the excessive privileges of the priesthood and set out to destroy church hierarchy. It put forward the revolutionary notion of a universal priesthood: "our baptism makes us all priests." And it demolished the "walls" behind which, Luther argued, Rome sat, fat and satisfied, in its spiritual and temporal power. Nevertheless, in tone his tract did not exile its author to the wilderness far outside of the church, but rather presented him as a biting and effective critic of priestly abuse. As if to titillate, Luther signaled at the end of this first treatise what was coming next: "I know another little song about Rome, and if their ears itch to hear it, I will sing it for them and will pitch it in a high key. Doest thou take my meaning, beloved Rome?"

The second, *The Freedom of a Christian*, the most lyrical of the three, heaped yet more contempt on the Holy See and personalized the attack by addressing the pope directly and contemptuously. "You, Leo, are like a lamb in the midst of wolves, like Daniel among the lions, or Ezekiel among the scorpions. . . . I truly despise your See, the Roman Curia, which neither you nor anyone else can deny is more corrupt than any Babylon or Sodom that was ever conceived, for it is defined by completely depraved, hopeless, and notorious godlessness."

The third tract, called *The Babylonian Captivity of the Church*, was the most dangerous, for it set out to undermine the very core of Catholic belief—the seven sacraments—and it marked Luther's final, irreversible, irreparable, and irrevocable break with Rome. Henry decided to focus on *The Babylonian Captivity*.

In it Luther had compared Rome to Babylon, the Devil's city, the site in Scripture that stood in opposition to Jerusalem, the city of God. Just as the Jews of Jerusalem had been sold into captivity under the tyranny of the Babylonian Empire, so Christians were captive under the tyranny of Rome, which misused the seven sacraments to keep believers in virtual bondage. Luther denied that five of these supposed sacraments—marriage, confirmation, confession, the ordination of priests, extreme unction, and, of course, indulgences—were actually sacraments at all. Only the Eucharist and baptism were the true sacraments, and he devoted more than half his book to those.

The first way the church kept its followers in captivity was by giving priests the ability to deny the cup of wine to the masses. "Priests are not lords but servants," Luther wrote.

The second mode of captivity was the doctrine of transubstantiation, where in the Catholic liturgy the bread and wine actually become the body and blood of Christ in the celebration of the Eucharist. This Luther called "a monstrous word and a monstrous idea." To him, how one interpreted the passage in 1 Corinthians—"Take, eat, this is my body which was shed for you. Do this in remembrance of me" (11:24–25)—should be a matter of choice. "No one should fear being called a heretic if he believes that real bread and real wine are present on the altar," Luther wrote. "Everyone should feel at liberty to ponder, hold, and believe either one view or the other without endangering his salvation."

And the third type of captivity was to him the most wicked of all. Its misuse lay in treating the Mass as a sacrifice to be purchased from priests, whereby the ceremony becomes a profit-making enterprise. Its wares "are bought and sold, traded and bartered in the church. On these the priests and monks depend for their entire livelihood." In Luther's belief, viewing the Mass as a sacrifice put the emphasis on God's supposed anger at bad behavior rather than on his gift of grace, and it made priests the arbiters of salvation, toting up the good and bad deeds of a parishioner's life, and rendering a decision on salvation or damnation. Salvation was, in Luther's contrary view, the province solely of the divine, and God's gift of salvation would be based solely on faith. In short, viewing the Mass as sacrifice encouraged fear of divine retribution rather than inviting genuine atonement, given freely and voluntarily.

Luther's attack on the Catholic Mass, especially transubstantiation, went deeper than his abhorrence of the entrepreneurial aspects of the ritual. The link between Christ's sacrifice at Calvary and the ritual of the Last Supper, as it was manifest in the Eucharist, stretched back to the second century. After the Diet of Worms, his excommunication by the church, and the imperial ban by Charles V, however, Luther was prohibited from discharging the privileges of a priest. Before Worms, he had celebrated a Mass every day; now at Wartburg, he was barred from this holiest and most precious of all priestly duties. And so, arguably, for personal reasons, he had set out to undermine the significance of the Eucharist, to downplay and demystify its magic. If he could not officiate at the mystical transformation of the bread and wine into the body and blood of Christ, let him doubt that this real presence existed at all.

Henry's attack on *The Babylonian Captivity* was swift. In the weeks after the Diet of Worms, a book called *Assertio Septem Sacramentorum* or *The Defense of the Seven Sacraments* was produced with Henry VIII claimed as its author. Indeed, Henry probably had written most of it, for there is evidence that the king had been scribbling feverishly at something or other during this period. But he certainly had ample help from Wolsey and Sir Thomas More, as well as John Fisher, the bishop of Rochester, and his own chaplain, Edward Lee. By one historian's account, Henry enjoyed reading purple passages of his prose to his advisers. Once, it was said, More objected to the king's overwrought tone. "Your Grace should be guarded in your expressions," More cautioned. "One day the Pope may be opposed to England, and here is a passage wherein you exalt the authority of the Holy See into too high a pitch."

"No, no," the king replied. "That expression is by no means too strong. Nothing can equal my devotion to the Holy See, and no language can be sufficiently expressive to speak my sentiments."

"But sire, do you not remember certain articles in the statute of *Praemunire?*" More said, referring to the statute from the time of Richard II that restrained papal intervention into the affairs of England.

"What matter," scoffed Henry. "Do I not hold my crown from the Holy See?"

When the king's *Assertio* came to Luther's attention many months later, he concluded that the good Reverend Lee had done most of the dirty work. "There are some who believe that Henry is not the author of the work," Luther would write. "My opinion is that King Henry perhaps gave one or two yards of cloth to Lee, and that Lee had made thereof a cape, to which he has sewn in a lining. What is there so wonderful in a King of England having written against me? If a King of England spits forth his lying insults in my face, I have the right, in self-defense, to thrust them down his throat."

Trading insults was the game now, and Henry rose to the contest with gusto. Luther was "a venomous serpent, a pernicious plague, an infernal wolf, an infectious soul, a detestable trumpeter of pride, calumnies, and schism, having an execrable mind, a filthy tongue, a detestable touch, stuffed with venom. This hideous monster having been caught will become benumbed with his own vermin." One can imagine the jolly king reading that line out loud to Wolsey and More. To put a fine point on the matter, Henry wrote to Charles V on May 20, just as Luther was settling in at the Wartburg, calling the scoundrel "this weed, this dilapidated, sick, and evil-minded sheep."

The effrontery of a simple friar espousing these terrible ideas galled the king. A personal peeve was Luther's attack on St. Thomas Aquinas and the Thomists. Aquinas's beautifully bound works occupied a prominent place in the king's library, and Henry read and reread the saint's works often. Luther had concealed his "Satanic malice" under the cloak of a zeal for the truth. With a sidelong glance toward the Vatican, Henry wrote, "Who is he, this single, insignificant monk, to challenge the majestic tribunal of the Saints, the Fathers, and the Popes? How could Luther expect that anybody should believe that all nations, cities, kingdoms and provinces should be so prodigal of their rights and liberties as to acknowledge the superiority of a strange priest to whom they owe no allegiance?"

But the king despaired of a recantation from such a creature. "Alas, the most greedy wolf of hell has surprised him, devoured and swallowed him down into the lowest part of his belly where he lies half alive, and half dead. And while the pious pastor calls him and bewails his loss, he belches out of the filthy mouth of the hellish wolf this foul inveighing which the ears of the whole flock do detest, disdain, and abhor."

Besides mockery and insult, the king tried pity as a weapon against his villain. Speaking as if Luther stood before him as a guilty wretch in his royal court, Henry wrote, "Oh, unhappy man! Do you not understand how far superior obedience is to sacrifice? Do you not see that if the sentence of death be uttered in the book of Deuteronomy against every man that dares to disobey a priest his master, how you merit—yes, justly merit—every imaginable punishment for having disobeyed the priest of priests?"

In his *Assertio*, Henry had a parting shot, casting Luther as an elusive, evil Proteus: "What good can result from a contest with Luther who agrees with none, who understands not himself, who denies what he at first asserted, asserts what he had but just denied. If you buckle on the armor of faith to resist him, he runs to reason. If you appeal to reason, he flies to faith. If you quote the philosophers, he appeals to Holy Writ. If you follow him there, he loses himself in the labyrinth of the sophisms of the schools. An audacious writer, who puts himself above all love, despises

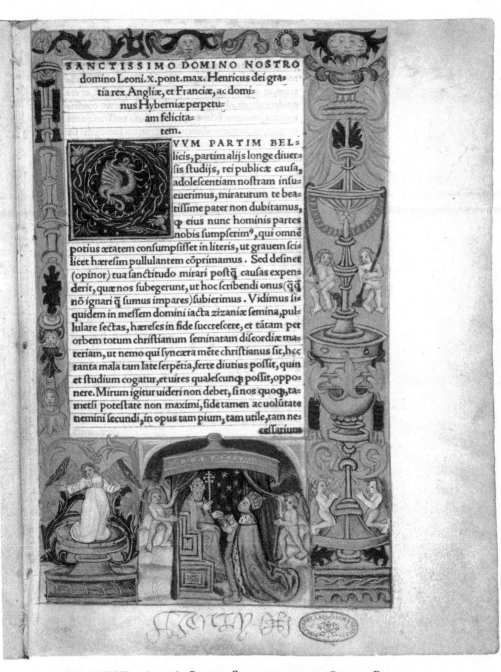

Henry VIII's *Assertio Septem Sacramentorum*. Credit: Biblioteca Apostolica Vaticana

our doctors and from his pinnacle of arrogance laughs at the living lights of our Church and insults the majesty of our Pontiff's traditions, dogmas, orals, canons, the faith, and even the Church herself."

Reflecting the pride of its author, Henry's *Assertio* was printed in bold Latin script. Its title page bore the arms of England encircled with flowers. The title page featured the image of a curtain being drawn back as the pope sits on his throne holding a copy of the *Assertio* and, before him, Henry on bended knee. The book was bound in golden cloth and taken to Rome by an English ambassador. On the first and last page of the text, Henry wrote a couplet in his own hand: "*Anglorum Rex Henricus, Leo Decime, mittit hoc opus et fidei et testem amicitie*," or "Henry, King of the English, sends this work to Leo X as a witness of faith and friendship."

Attached to the manuscript was a lengthy letter postmarked May 21, 1521, from the Royal Palace at Greenwich. When he learned of the "pest of Martin Luther's heresy" and understood its "deadly venom," the king explained to Leo, he was so aggrieved that he felt compelled to wonder how he might uproot these scurrilous whimsies from the Lord's flock. Learned and scholarly men from all parts of his realm had examined its errors, the king wrote. He had determined to employ his "modest ability" to show by his own writing a worthy condemnation of these "vile books." He dedicated the work to His Holiness "as a token of his filial reverence."

Lest the pope overlook what Henry really wanted from his valiant efforts, his ambassador stressed the motto of Henry's England, "One God, One Baptism, One Faith!" and said that no country hated Luther and his heresies more than his beloved island kingdom. The diplomat emphasized that the work was sent in the hope that "all might see that the King of England is ready to defend the church not only with his arms, but with the resources of his mind." An extravagant event for the book's presentation was suggested in which the king hoped he would, at last, receive the coveted title of "defender of the faith."

"I might hope," continued the ambassador, "that what the Godly Prince has writ against Luther's errors might compel Luther himself (if he has the least spark of Christian piety left in him) to recant his heresies and recall again the straying and almost forlorn sheep. But what can be done when Pharaoh's heart is hardened? Where the wound stings with putrefaction? Truly my most serene king is not expecting any good from this idle and vain phantom. He rather thinks this raging and mad dog is not to be dealt with by words."

Through the summer of 1521 the pope evaded Henry's request for a formal presentation of his *Assertio*, since in the wake of the Diet of Worms he did not want to stir up Protestant frenzy in Germany further. But in October Leo X relented, and the desired presentation went forward. At the unveiling the flattery was extravagant. One Vatican prelate compared Henry to King Solomon, while Leo himself extolled the book's "eloquence of style." Giving thanks to the Creator, "who has raised such a prince to defend his Holy Church and this Holy See," the pope praised the king for "the knowledge, will, and ability to compose this book against this terrible monster." As a final touch, the pope promised an indulgence to anyone who read Henry's book. (Lucky for Leo that he was not still alive five years later, when Henry VIII came running to the Vatican to annul his marriage to Catherine of Aragon.)

Back in Germany, Henry's *Assertio* also found an audience. Elector Frederick's cousin Duke George of Saxony, Luther's archenemy, caused Henry's rant to be translated and published in German. At last Luther could swallow the whole cloth, and on August 4 he sent his answer.

In the back of his mind as he composed his response may have been the line from Psalm 119:46, which often appears on Luther statuary: "I will speak of thy testimonies also before kings, and will not be ashamed."

If Henry thought himself to be the master of insult, he met his match. And if he thought the simple monk would be intimidated by a king, he was mistaken, for to Luther Henry VIII was a secondary monarch who had no power to threaten him. It is doubtful that Luther would have dared to curse the first monarchs of Europe, Charles V or Francis I, with such an epithet as "impudent liar," for these potentates were far more dangerous to him. But he showed no such restraint in dealing with the English king.

"What a fool!" Luther wrote of Henry. "One might suppose that a declared enemy of the king had written the book to bring everlasting disgrace upon himself." To level things, Junker Jörg came to refer to the king as "Junker Heintz."

Among the many slurs in Henry's book was the charge that Luther had been inconsistent, and this seemed to gall Luther more than anything. If he changed his positions occasionally, whose opinions did not evolve over time? Luther wondered. "Here the miserable scribbler has demonstrated with poisonous words how well he can manage to soil a lot of paper, a truly royal deed," he wrote. "From now on, no Christian can any longer improve himself or do penance because the Kings of England would come along and say, 'Look, they confess as sin and error what formerly they maintained to be good and right.' I wonder whether so clever a king keeps wearing his children's shoes, which after all are a contradiction of the shoes a grown man wears. How can he nowadays drink wine, considering there was a time when he was sucking milk?"

The verbal joust between Luther and the king left a lasting impression on the Reformer, imparting to him an even greater contempt for the high and the mighty. In the tract *Temporary*

Authority: To What Extent It Can Be Obeyed, published two years later, he wrote: "Since the beginning of the world a wise prince is a mighty rare bird, and an upright prince even rarer. They are generally the biggest fools or the worst scoundrels on earth. One must constantly expect the worst from them and look for little good. They are God's executioners and hangmen." With regularity Luther would invoke the fairy tale about the conceited frog who longs to be as big and scary as an ox, so he inflates himself bigger and bigger until he bursts with a bang. At the noise, the ox raises his head when he hears the pop and then goes back to his drinking. The other frogs hop away, croaking, "It doesn't do to become too swollen-headed."

It was a lesson of which Luther himself might take heed.

Nor was the contest quickly forgotten in England. The riposte to Luther's rebuttal was delegated to Sir Thomas More, the distinguished author and privy councilor and, years later, victim himself of Henry's ire. In a tract of more than three hundred pages called *Responsio ad Lutherum*, published in 1523, he called Luther "a pig, a dolt, and a liar," an "ape," "drunkard," "a pestilential buffoon," and "lousy little friar." Luther's writings, wrote the judicious Sir Thomas, came from snippets he had gleaned in brothels, barber shops, taverns, and privies. In his notebooks the monk wrote down anything he heard when a coachman spoke "ribaldly," or a servant "insolently," or "a whore wantonly," or a pimp "indecently," or a bath-keeper "filthily," or a shitter "obscenely." And then, as if he had not got his point across sufficiently, More lost his literary and lawyerly composure entirely when he wrote, "For as long as your reverend paternity is determined to tell these shameless lies, others are permitted on behalf of his English majesty, to throw back into your paternity's shitty mouth, truly the shit-pool of all shit, all the muck and shit which your damnable rottenness has vomited up."

By this time events had long since overtaken the royal pique, and no one was paying attention to More's tirade. There was a new pope in Rome, and partly inspired by Luther, Germany was lurching toward class warfare between peasants and lords. And in another fourteen years More himself would be subjected to the anger of Henry VIII when he refused to go along with the annulment of Henry's marriage to Catherine of Aragon and his marriage to Anne Boleyn. Specifically, More balked at the act of succession that transferred the succession to the throne from the children of Catherine to the children of Anne. For this More paid with his life and would come to be known as the "Reformation martyr."

And perhaps most interesting of all, by that time Henry VIII had done an about-face and had come running to Luther for support in his efforts for either divorce or bigamy.

Six

UNCLEAN THOUGHTS, DEVOURING FIRES

IN THE EARLY DAYS OF LUTHER'S SOJOURN AT THE WARTBURG, before he settled into his frantic pace of work, he seemed to lapse into a delirious, mystical state. The serenity of the landscape, the call of the nightingale, the joy of isolation, the freedom from fear, the distance from harassing inquisitors—all these presaged a time when he would be more productive in his theological and literary output than at any other period of his life.

It is not surprising that in his solitude the natural and unnatural, the healthy and unhealthy physical life of a human being should have come into his thoughts. That process would lead him to ponder again the question of priestly celibacy and to deliberate on his own sexuality and on carnal drives in general.

On May 19, he touched on the subject of physical love in a letter to Nicolas Gerbel, a jurist, doctor of canon law, and humanist from Strasbourg who would become an important supporter in subsequent battles and was deeply interested in Luther's literary life. It is not clear just how the two had first established their friendship or when Luther had met Gerbel and his wife. But from this letter it's evident that in Gerbel's marriage the Reformer perceived a romantic model. "Kiss and rekiss your wife," Luther wrote. "Let her love and be loved. You are fortunate in having overcome, by an honorable marriage, that celibacy in which one is a prey to devouring fires and to unclean ideas. That unhappy state of a single person, male or female, reveals to me each hour of the day so many horrors, that nothing sounds in my ear as bad as the name of monk or nun or priest. A married life is a paradise, even where all else is wanting."

Inevitably, he found biblical validation for the sporting that goes on between husband and wife. "We are permitted to laugh and have fun with and embrace our wives, whether they are naked or clothed," just as Isaac fondled his wife in Genesis 26:8. (Later he would refer to sex between spouses as precious and beneficial.) And female companionship was an excellent antidote to a man's melancholy. "When you are assailed by gloom, despair or a trouble conscience, you should eat, drink, and talk with others. If you can find help for yourself by thinking of a girl, do so."

Luther had treated the subject of marriage in his Babylonian captivity essay. While he proclaimed marriage to be a divine institution—"What therefore God hath joined together, let not man put asunder" (Matthew 19:6)—he denied that the institution was a sacrament. A sacrament, he insisted, was a mystery, a secret rite, a visible sign of spiritual grace that came from God not humans. The human laws that extolled marriage had actually turned it into a "farce," he wrote. These "shameful laws" made priests into merchants who were "selling vulvas and genitals" through greed and godlessness. "The laws of men seem to have sprung into existence as snares for taking money and nets for catching souls . . . openly selling the pudenda of both sexes." If a couple in love know divine law and had natural wisdom, he noted, then "written laws will be entirely superfluous and harmful. Above all, love needs no laws whatever."

Nowhere in the Bible was the celibacy of priests commanded nor their marriage forbidden, he insisted. Indeed, the contrary was true. He pointed out that James (the first martyred apostle) and all the apostles except John were married, and that the Bible portrays Paul as a widower. He invoked Paul's letters to Timothy and to Titus: a bishop must be blameless and be husband to only one wife. The first prohibition of marriage was proclaimed in the year 385 by Pope Siricus, and it was done out of "sheer wantonness."

Worse than wantonness, it was the work of the Devil, Luther argued, for it increased sin, shame, and scandal without end. Prohibiting prelates from marital bliss was the effusion of the Anti-Christ. Again he invoked Paul's First Letter to Timothy: "There shall come false prophets, seducing spirits, speaking lies in hypocrisy, forbidding marriage" (1 Timothy 4:1–4). Of the priest who takes a secret lover, Luther said, "his conscience is troubled, yet no one does anything to help him, though he might easily be helped." Moreover, the controversy had led to the catastrophic schism between the Eastern and Western churches in the eleventh century. In the eastern Greek Orthodox Church the priest was required to marry a woman for the good of his community and himself. Luther seemed to like that idea, and he proposed that every Christian community appoint a pious and learned person as a minister, leaving him free to marry or not.

For biblical certification he continued to rely on Paul's First Epistle to Timothy. According to 1 Timothy 3:2–3, the institution was specifically sanctioned: "A bishop then must be blameless, the husband of one wife, vigilant, sober, of good behaviour, given to hospitality, apt to teach; not given to wine, no striker, not greedy of filthy lucre; but patient, not a brawler, not covetous."

Most of all, he denied that this or any other pope had any standing whatever to legislate human sexuality. "Does the pope set up laws?" he had asked in his essay on the church's Babylonian captivity. "Let him set them up for himself and keep hands off my liberty." If a priest was supposed to be celibate, what standing did he have to set up rules about sex for the laity?

But Luther did not stop there. He ventured unhesitatingly into areas where even a layperson much less a priest feared to tread: into questions of adultery, impotence, fornication, and masturbation. What was a wife to do when she found herself married to an impotent husband? Luther's answer: she should seek a divorce and marry one more suitable and satisfying. But what if the impotent husband should not agree? Luther's answer: then with the sufferance of her husband—he was not really a husband anyway, but merely the man dwelling with her under the same roof—she should have intercourse with another, perhaps the husband's brother, and the children from such a union should be regarded as rightful heirs.

And should a spouse wish to obtain a divorce, what about the Catholic law against remarriage? Luther answered that he or she should be permitted to remarry: "Yet it is still a greater wonder to me why they compel a man to remain unmarried after being separated from his wife by divorce, and why they will not permit him to remarry. For if Christ permits divorce on the ground of fornication (Matthew 5:32) and compels no one to remain unmarried . . . then he certainly seems to permit a man to marry another woman in the place of the one who has been put away."

But what about the Catholic Church's prohibition of divorce, all divorce? "The tyranny of the laws permits no divorce," Luther wrote. "But the woman is free through the divine law and cannot be compelled to suppress her carnal desires. Therefore the man ought to concede her right and give up to somebody else the wife who is his only in outward appearance." Still he detested divorce, he insisted, and preferred bigamy, considering it the lesser of evils and validated by multiple stories in the Old Testament. And annulment? Well, that process was far too complicated and time-consuming, not to mention the toll it took on all the parties.

But then came the Roman See, fumed Luther, and forbade priests to marry with no just foundation, and this had increased "division, sin, shame, and scandal to be increased without end." It had led priests into irresistible temptation. The ban, therefore, was the work of the Devil, and to demand a vow of celibacy at the consecration of a priest was "the Devil's own tyranny."

The Vatican of Leo X and the Church of England under a youthful Henry VIII took violent exception to Luther's view of marriage, dubbing it a sensualized code of ethics, little removed from paganism. That Henry VIII would take upon himself the role of defending the sanctity of marriage was rich in irony, of course, for it would not be many years hence before the king would seek out Luther's support in his quest for annulment, divorce, and bigamy. Given what was to come later, one can only titter with delight in reading Henry's self-righteousness: "Whom God has joined let no man put asunder. Who does not tremble when he considers how to deal with his wife?" The king quoted St. Augustine: "The sacrament of marriage is common to all nations. But the sanctity of it is only in the City of our God, and in his holy mountain (the Church)."

"And so I say," Luther wrote of a priest and a woman he loved, "let him take and keep her as his wedded wife, and live honestly with her as her husband, caring nothing whether the pope will have it so or not, whether it be against canon law or human law. The salvation of your soul is of more importance than tyrannical, arbitrary, wicked laws which are not necessary for salvation and are not commanded by God."

IMAGO MARTINI LVTHERI EO HABITV EX PRESSA, QVO REVERSVS EST EX PATHMO WITENBERGAM, ANNO DOMINI 1 5 2 2.

Luther as Junker Jörg. By Lucas Cranach the Elder. CREDIT: NATIONAL GALLERY OF ART, WASHINGTON

Already, as Luther languished at the Wartburg, a number of priests were taking this advice and marrying by the score.

ONLY A FEW DAYS OF HIS ARRIVAL AT THE WARTBURG, THE Reformer was brought low with a terrible, immobilizing case of gastrointestinal distress. Severe physical pain in his lower regions tormented him and added to his delirium. While in mind and spirit he desperately wanted to focus on lofty matters of faith and the church, the demands of his body drew him back to more elemental matters.

"The elimination is so hard that I'm forced to press with all my strength, even to the point of perspiration. The longer I delay the worse it gets," he wrote to Melanchthon on May 12. "This affliction will be intolerable if it continues as it has begun."

By early summer he still had no relief. "The Lord has overwhelmed me," he moaned. "Excrements are so hard that push with much force I am driven to the point of sweat. And the longer I am disturbed, the more they grow hard. Lately, they were excreted only on the fourth day." His debilitated state led him to feel as if his God and his friends had forsaken him. If his principles made him stop short of blaming God directly for his discomfort, he heaped scorn on his closest friend.

His correspondence with Melanchthon became increasingly overwrought. If he did not hear from his confidante daily, he felt abandoned by him. Frustrated at the slow pace at which his writings were being published, he berated his disciple for a series of real or imagined slights. Melanchthon was both too remote and too fawning, Luther complained. The young man was working too hard, even though Luther had cautioned him against it. "Here you are being led by your own stubbornness. I shout this at you often, but it is as if I am shouting to someone who is deaf."

He scolded Melanchthon roundly, as if the little Greek were a callow, fawning youth. "You give in too much to your emotions, and, as is your way, you are just too gentle. You extol me too much. You err tremendously in ascribing such great importance to me. Your opinion of me shames and tortures me."

Conflicting sentiments assailed him. He wanted to feel needed in Wittenberg. One moment he was expressing satisfaction at

how well things were going there and complimented Melanchthon on how he was managing in his absence. "You are already
replacing me," he wrote in a tone that was both baiting and
needy. "Because of the gifts you have from God, you have attained greater authority and popularity than me." The next moment he was lashing out at his persecutors, high and low, friend
or foe, real or imagined. It was as if this tormented genius, so concerned about love, loving, and being loved, had given himself
over to hate and resentment.

Even those who were going to extraordinary lengths to make
him feel safe and comfortable came in for his disparagement.
He was pampered with unaccustomed luxury, yet he belittled
his guardians. "I believe it is the prince who pays," he wrote to
George Spalatin, about their mutual benefactor, Elector Frederick, "for I would not remain an hour here, if I were not living
at the expense of my host. If it is the prince's bread, let it be.
For if one must consume the fortune of any one, it ought to be
the fortune of princes, since prince and rogue are terms nearly
synonymous." His contempt for princes, even Frederick, trumped
the need for gratitude. Princes were "great fools, great rascals, the
jailers and executioners of God," but their bread was good.

On July 13, in a letter to Melanchthon, he announced that
he had neither prayed nor studied nor written anything for eight
days. "This is partly because of temptations of the flesh," he
wrote, "partly because I am tortured by other burdens." (His con-
stipation, he confided, was brought on by a lesion in his anus.) If
things did not improve, he threatened to go to Erfurt ("and not
incognito") to see surgeons, even if it meant capture and martyrdom. Then they would be sorry. "I cannot endure this evil any
longer," he said pitiably. "It would be easier to endure ten big
wounds than this small lesion. Maybe the Lord burdens me so as
to push me out of this hermitage into the public."

Luther's threat was hollow, for Erfurt remained in the firm control of the Catholic authorities. Its city council, it must be remembered, had suppressed violent student riots after Luther's visit there on the way to Worms, and several wayward priests had been excommunicated. If Luther were apprehended in Erfurt now, things would go badly for him. In any event, he soon learned that black plague had broken out in Erfurt, and this provided a ready excuse to stop his empty fulminations.

"Of course, this plague will be charged to us on the grounds that we heretics have provoked God, and we will be scorned by men and despised by the people," Luther remarked.

If he blamed others for his situation, he also blamed himself. He was sinking into self-pity and self-loathing. "I sit here like a fool and hardened in leisure, pray little, do not care for the Church of God, yet burn in a big fire of my untamed body," he lamented. "I should be ardent in spirit, but I am ardent in the flesh, in lust, laziness, effeminacy, and sleepiness. I do not know whether God has turned away from me, since you all do not pray for me."

In short, Martin Luther was becoming a very difficult man.

He was entering the dangerous territory of priestly temptation, as it related to celibacy, chastity, and clerical vows. A year earlier, in his essay *To the Christian Nobility of the German Nation*, he had called the celibacy of priests "wretched" and the monk's vow of chastity "Devilish tyranny." But his writing on the subject then, among the conviviality of friends, had the feel of abstraction. Now in his isolation and his physical suffering, he was experiencing lust and fire in his loins viscerally and intensely.

Inevitably he turned to the Bible for instruction, especially Paul's First Epistle to the Corinthians. From that he drew the conclusion that the benefits of marriage overshadowed the advantages of celibacy, from a spiritual point of view.

To isolate priests from women was—for most—impossible to bear, he had come to believe. The idea that abstinence from sex, celibacy, privation, and self-torture insured salvation was a myth. In the monastery he had been taught that to be in the cloister, making a trip to Rome or Santiago de Compostella, and living a severe life of denial, led to God's grace. That was nonsense, he felt now. Even providing priests with female housekeepers was a dangerous practice. "It is like putting straw and fire together and forbidding them to smoke or burn," he would write later. And it was common in those days to lay the blame for priestly abuse on the women, by calling convents sexual hothouses, where predatory, lusty women were lurking behind their walls, waiting to pounce on any innocent male who turned up.

At last, in late July, Luther got some relief from his physical, if not his psychological, distress. George Spalatin, the chaplain to Elector Frederick, sent him medication from the court apothecary, and these pills, most likely a purgative compound of vegetable extracts of rhubarb and senna pods laced with opium, seemed to provide some relief. In a thank-you note, Luther wrote to the chaplain, "I had some relief and elimination without blood or force, but the wound of the previous rupture isn't healed yet. I even had to suffer a good deal because some flesh extruded, either due to the power of the pills, or I don't know what. So I shall wait once more and see."

Two weeks later, the refugee was feeling better. Writing again to Spalatin he said, "I have easier elimination now, due to your strong and powerful medications, but the way my digestion functions has not changed at all. The soreness continues, and I am afraid it may develop into a worse evil with which the Lord afflicts me, according to his wisdom."

ACROSS GERMANY RUMORS ABOUT LUTHER CONTINUED TO fly. Besides those who were sure he was dead, others had heard that he resided in a secret place in the underworld and was communicating with invisible spirits and was even having nocturnal colloquies with the Devil himself.

One rumor would get special carriage then and later. In Ingolstadt in the devoutly Catholic region of Bavaria, lived a young woman named Argula von Stauff, who hailed from a prominent, well-educated family of free persons called Berlips. Stauff was the beneficiary of a fine intellectual and religious education, unusual for girls of the time. At the age of sixteen she repaired to the court of Munich, where she was a lady-in-waiting to the daughter of Emperor Frederick III. In 1516 she married a noble from a family somewhat lower in station than her own.

When Luther's works began to be widely and secretly distributed in Catholic lands, Argula von Stauff read them avidly and obsessively. Somehow she heard that after the Diet of Worms the Reformer was holed up in the Wartburg Castle, and she declared her intention to meet the great man. With her docile husband's sufferance, she traveled to Eisenach. At this point the tale receives some embroidering. The captain of the castle, Hans von Berlepsch, it is said, admitted the supplicant graciously, but informed her that Junker Jörg was then busy in a different part of the castle and could not be disturbed. (His unavailability, so the story goes, was due to the fact that he was then dueling with the Devil himself.) But the accommodating von Berlepsch allowed Stauff to sleep in Luther's bed alone. It was not to be a restful stay, for throughout the night there was a terrible clatter, as if surely Satan inhabited the premises. The next day Stauff beat a hasty retreat.

As the story is told in Catholic rendering, when Luther returned from his combat with the Devil and was told that the lady slept in his bed, he wrote, "My indomitable flesh boils and is on fire."

Luther consigned these nocturnal urgings to the Devil, who sat by his pillow and sent titillating dreams that covered his face with perspiration. In recognizing and acknowledging these urges, Luther was suffering from his own pollution, as he saw it, a pollution that denied him the possibility to be pure according to Catholic ritual.

He was allowing his mind to go places it had never gone before. Since his mind would not allow him to abstain from these "devouring thoughts," he wallowed in them in order to understand them, which led him to see the contradiction in the demand of celibacy and question the validity of the imperative toward purity and abstinence for priests.

There is an indisputable footnote to the Argula von Stauff story. She was to become a very substantial woman, the first notable Protestant woman writer who went on to publish widely read letters and poems and became a fierce defender of Lutheranism. Two years after her supposed journey to Luther's bed, she became embroiled in a controversy over an eighteen-year-old student and teacher at the University of Ingolstadt who was arrested for his Lutheran views and forced to recant. Stauff rose fiercely to his defense.

In a letter to the rector of the faculty, she wrote: "What have Luther and Melanchthon taught save the Word of God? You have condemned them. You have not refuted them. Where do you read in the Bible that Christ, the apostles, and the prophets imprisoned, banished, burned, or murdered anyone? You tell us that we must obey the magistrates. Correct. But neither the pope, nor the Kaiser, nor the princes have any authority over the Word of God. You need not think you can pull God, the prophets and the apostles out of heaven with papal decrees.

"You seek to destroy all of Luther's works. In that case you will have to destroy the New Testament. . . . But you are defeating yourselves. The news of what has been done to this lad has reached us and other cities in so short a time that soon it will be known to all the world. The Lord will forgive this young man, and great good will yet come from him. I send you not a woman's ranting, but the Word of God. I write as a member of the Church of Christ against which the gates of hell shall not prevail."

For her public protest she would be called a "shameless whore" and a "female desperado." For a woman to mount such a direct attack on the Catholic Church in that day and age was extraordinary.

In 1530 Argula von Stauff finally met Luther face to face, but there is no account of what was said or what was remembered.

Seven

RIVALS SURFACE

IN MIDSUMMER OF 1521, NEWS CAME TO LUTHER THAT HIS hideout might have been inadvertently disclosed in dangerous quarters. A secretary to Duke John the Steady, Frederick's brother and co-ruler in Thuringia, had casually written to a friend and revealed Luther's whereabouts at the Wartburg. This dangerous breach of secrecy was conveyed to Luther by his attentive minder, Hans von Berlepsch, who said that the rumor was gaining credence and spreading rapidly. Satan was at work in this mischief, Luther was convinced. "Up until now we have bravely kept our secret," he said. "I'm indignant that our undertakings should be so easily made fruitless."

The revelation rattled Luther and punctured his posturing. To deflect the damage, the Reformer retreated into adolescent subterfuge. Writing to George Spalatin, he enclosed a false letter in his own handwriting, intended to put the hounds of Rome off the scent. "Listen to my ruse," he wrote, as if he were whispering. "When the rumor of my whereabouts becomes strong, I want you to 'lose' the enclosed letter. This should be done with studied carelessness in a stealthy way, so that the letter falls into the hands of the Hog of Dresden"—his moniker for Duke George, his most dangerous enemy.

The false letter was addressed to Spalatin. "I hear a rumor is being spread that Luther is living in the Wartburg near Eisenach," it read. "This is understandable since I was captured in the forest near there. But I am hidden far away in safety, provided that the friars around me keep the secret. If the books I am publishing betray me, I shall move my quarters. Strange that nobody now thinks of Bohemia." Bohemia?

But the Reformer was a better preacher than spymaster. His lame effort at disinformation, suggesting that he was hiding in a Bohemian monastery somewhere, had a certain plausibility. Bohemia was the font of heresy, the place where Jan Huss had lived and was burned a century earlier for arguing that a communicant at the Eucharist should be given both bread and wine, rather than bread alone. This was precisely the position that Luther was now arguing as well. Heretics flock together, don't they?

Initially, Cardinal Aleander had indeed suggested to the Roman Curia that Bohemia was Luther's likely place of refuge. By naively mentioning the Wartburg specifically as the place where he was not, however, the first thing any good detective would have done with such a negative suggestion was to check there first. Fortunately, Spalatin did not have to pursue this nonsense. The letters were never distributed.

Meanwhile in Wittenberg, during the early summer months of 1521, Luther's rivals began to assert themselves. A group of Augustinians led by a friar named Gabriel Zwilling was contemplating radical changes in the Mass. All private, profit-making Masses, for which priests charged handsome sums, might be eliminated altogether. In the public mass at Wittenberg, both bread and wine were already being offered at communion, contrary to the Vatican injunction against wine. There was discussion as to whether the host should be "elevated" to heaven by the priest during the Eucharist. Symbols of piety like crucifixes, statues of saints, and icons ought to be removed from the church. Should priests really wear their fancy vestments at the altar rather than a simple robe? And why should the Mass be said in Latin rather than German? Why should the words of the Eucharist be whispered rather than shouted to the rafters? Luther would come to refer to these militants as *schwärmer* or the "enthusiasts." To him it was premature to press such reforms, especially in his absence and without his sanction.

The politics of the Reformation were becoming radicalized beyond Luther's desires, and he was losing control. If the Wittenberg crowd moved too fast, he felt it could threaten the ultimate success of his movement. But he was too far away to stop or slow down the novelties.

A larger threat presented itself in the person of Luther's colleague at Wittenberg University, the theologian named Andreas Karlstadt. Three years younger than Luther, but superior to him as dean of the Wittenberg faculty and chancellor of the university, Karlstadt was a man of great learning with a fearless and intrepid temperament. (It was he who had conferred Luther's doctorate.) They had worked closely together in the confrontation with Rome in 1517—Karlstadt had nailed his own theses to the door of the Wittenberg Church in that year, fifty more complaints than Luther—and together they had appeared in disputations with various apologists whom Rome had sent to Germany. Leo X's bull *Ex Surge Domine* had also excommunicated Karlstadt.

Until Luther's disappearance, the two had been comrades in holy combat. Now, in Luther's absence, Karlstadt moved to seize control of the reform movement. Even before Luther went to Worms, his rival had condemned prayers for the dead and

Luther and Jan Huss Give Communion to the Princes of Saxony.
CREDIT: NATIONAL GALLERY OF ART, WASHINGTON

demanded that the Mass be said in the vernacular German. At this point Luther had endorsed neither position. Then, as Luther was just getting settled in the Wartburg in mid-May, Karlstadt publicly questioned the very basis of the Eucharist and the need for the elevation of the host. He denounced the practice of withholding the chalice of wine from the laity, a view Luther did hold, but Karlstadt was co-opting Luther's leadership by announcing it.

Karlstadt was usurping Luther's preeminence in other ways. In early June he traveled to Denmark to advise the Danish king on the restraint of bishops, as that country moved toward its own reformed church. When he returned, he was full of his own eminence. "We must begin sometime or nothing will be done," he said, implying that Luther might be out of the picture for a very long time, perhaps forever. "He who puts his hand to the plough should not look back."

On June 21 Karlstadt held a disputation on clerical celibacy. In the conclave he questioned the rationale for the celibacy of priests and even, to Luther's initial dismay, of monks. (Luther regarded the commitment of monks to be stricter and more profound than the commitment of mere priests.) Both Luther and Karlstadt knew full well that many a priest was cavorting secretly with wife and child and, as such, was tormented by the "hot iron" of a bad conscience. But Karlstadt was getting out in front of Luther's strategy on the celibacy issue and pushing the Reformation into waters for which Luther felt the movement might not be prepared.

In his June 21 disputation Karlstadt wanted to take the matter even further. From his university conclave, he published his thoughts eight days later in a treatise entitled *On Celibacy, Monastic Life, and Widowhood*. "Based on biblical law or Holy Scripture," Karlstadt wrote, "priests, monks, and nuns who like one another can and should marry in good conscience and with God's will and enter into the marital state without asking for dispensation or permission from Rome, which is altogether unnecessary. Such persons should give up their hypocritical lives and enter fully into real Christian life." Karlstadt also argued that the betrothed clerics should give up their caps and cassocks as the price of marital bliss. This Luther could not accept.

On July 22 Karlstadt pushed a step further by removing all pictures, icons, and statuary in the Wittenberg town church.

In early August at the Wartburg, Luther finally received his rival's treatise on celibacy. During the weeks that followed, he seemed obsessed with the subject of sexuality. Contemplating his nighttime dreams, fantasies, sweats, and temptations, he would remember that even when he was old, St. Augustine complained of "nocturnal pollutions." When desire tormented St. Jerome, he beat his breast with stones but still was unable to drive the memory of the girl he had seen dancing in Rome out of his mind. To suppress desire, St. Francis had employed snowballs, and St. Benedict lay down on a bed of thorns. "If there are fluxes and pollutions, the gift of virginity is no longer there," Benedict would say later. "So the remedy of marriage which God has given should be embraced."

Passionately, Luther jumped on Karlstadt's work as an aberration. Karlstadt had chosen the wrong scriptural references for this issue, he felt, and those he had chosen he had twisted and misinterpreted to make his arguments. By such sloppiness, his colleague was damaging the movement. To Melanchthon Luther complained, "I don't want you at Wittenberg to be publishing anything based on obscure and ambiguous scriptural passages, since the light which is demanded of us has to be brighter than the sun and all the stars. And even then our enemies hardly see!" He applauded his rival for taking on a difficult subject, "but I wish it were done in a skillful and successful way. You see what great clarity our enemies demand of us, since they misrepresent even the most obvious of our statements."

The Reformer was especially offended by Karlstadt's remark that to command the chastity of a priest was like casting his semen as a sacrifice to Molech—the king of the Canaanites and Phoenicians to whom parents sacrificed their children in Leviticus 18:21 and 20:2. This was a veiled reference to masturbation. "Our enemies will ridicule the distortion of this passage," Luther warned Melanchthon, "since it is clear as day that it refers to the sons and daughters who were being sacrificed as a burnt offering to the idol," and not casting one's semen into the dirt.

Beyond the question of biblical misrepresentation, the "enthusiasts" in Wittenberg were entering the troublesome area of masturbation, homosexuality, and adultery. "Karlstadt is comparing the effeminate to Onan, the son of Judah. (Gen. 38:9)," Luther wrote to Melanchthon. "But that person did not spoil his seed in a passion, but with a wicked intent. It is not firmly established yet that effeminacy is a greater or lesser crime than fornication or adultery." Luther regarded onanism or masturbation to be immoral and a male's involuntary "nocturnal emissions" as unclean.

A few days later, the Reformer wrote again to Melanchthon: "I pity those poor girls and young men who are tormented in the flesh at night." And then, making fun of Karlstadt, he said, "Good God! Our Wittenbergers will end up giving a wife to every monk, but they shall not to me." (Not then, but maybe later.)

Thankfully, in this combat with Karlstadt, not every area of human sexuality was included in the debate. On homosexuality, the last frontier, Luther would evince no open-mindedness. Nor would he address the possibility that the incidence of homosexuality might come from the vows and laws that demanded total sexual abstinence of priests and monks. Luther identified homosexuality with the sin of Sodom, and his reference was Genesis 19:4–5. He saw it as a "monstrous depravity" and blamed Carthusian hermits of Italy for bringing the abomination into Germany. The people of Sodom had departed from the "natural longing" of the male for the female, he wrote. It was not mere unbridled, illicit lust, but divine ordinance that led to salvation. That "natural passion" was implanted in nature by God.

During his preoccupation with celibacy and carnal desires in early August, Luther himself was guilty of sloppiness, writing certain things that would later come back to haunt him. He held that man was born into sin, but that faith could triumph over sin. In a loose passage in an August 1 letter to Melanchthon, during a discussion of celibacy, he wrote: "Sin, and sin boldly, but let your faith be greater than your sin. . . . It is sufficient that we have known the Lamb of God who takes away the sins of the world. Sin cannot destroy in us the kingdom of the Lamb, even if we should fornicate and murder a million times daily."

Several years later when war broke out between peasants and nobles in Germany, this passage was interpreted as a call to licentiousness and would be used to justify horrific acts in the name of Luther and his God.

Eight

WRESTLING THE DEVIL

D URING LUTHER'S SEQUESTRATION AT THE WARTBURG Castle—as during his upbringing and his training as a priest, and long thereafter—the Devil was omnipresent in his life and faith. Powerful, crafty, subtle, moody, unpredictable, and very persistent, Satan was not easily discouraged or dispatched. Disease and plague were his handiwork. He possessed the blind, the mute, the mad, and the disabled. He was the author of night-mares and night sweats. He provoked wars and massacres. He was behind suicides: "It's the Devil who has put the cord around their neck or the knife to their throat," said Luther. When a man was found dead in his bed, it was Satan who had twisted his neck. Suicide was akin to being murdered in the forest by a robber, and the bandit was the Devil.

Human nature is to be happy and optimistic, Luther pro-claimed, but then the Devil comes along and "shits on him." Satan knew the thoughts of the wicked, since he was the one who had prompted those thoughts. He could pounce on the oc-cupants of a house, and "woe to him whom the Devil seizes in his fangs." Luther even knew of places in heaven and on earth where demons congregated. In heaven they resided on the dark edge of clouds. And on earth they were especially fond of Prussia. In Switzerland there was a lake high on a mountain called Pilate's Lake, where the Devil liked to play his pranks. And in the town of Poltersberg, the home of the noisy, mischievous poltergeist, there was a lake where, if you threw a stone into it, you could cause a great storm.

Through his religious training in Erfurt, Luther would have encountered Satan often in his biblical studies. He would have been taught that Lucifer, before his fall, had been chief of the archangels, but when God pushed him aside and appointed His son, Jesus, to supreme command over the heavenly host, Lucifer rebelled in disobedience and envy (Acts 13:10, 33), and for his sin of pride was cast out of heaven. In his anger he came down to earth in great wrath, where he became the angel of the Bottomless Pit (Revelation 9:11), the Red Dragon, the Beast, the Old Serpent, and the protester against Jesus called Legion (Mark 5:9). On earth, still possessing superhuman power, armed with subtle guile and boundless malice, Satan became humanity's enemy and tempter, a liar and slanderer, blind in his rage and unswerving in his grudge against God and humankind. His malice was equal to his power. Even as he was a true believer in God, he was indefatigable in his efforts to undermine God's church. He commanded an earthly apostate army of countless evil demons, and it is some of these Jesus exorcized at Gadara, putting them into the bodies of swine, whereupon the pigs raced down to the Sea of Galilee and drowned themselves (Mark 5:12–13; Luke 8:30).

By the time he arrived at the Wartburg, Luther had established a distinct intimacy with the Devil. Indeed, as he truly believed that the Devil caused thunder and lightning, he could give the Devil credit—or blame—for his conversion to the priesthood during the ferocious storm at Stotternheim in 1505. In the succeeding years he was tormented by his self-doubt, and especially in times when he was alone; the fallen angel visited him frequently.

"In our monastery in Wittenberg I heard him distinctly," Luther would remember later. "When I began to lecture on the Book of Psalms, and I was sitting in the refectory after we had sung matins, studying and writing my notes, the Devil came and thudded three times in the storage chamber, behind the stove, as if dragging a bushel away. Finally, as it did not want to stop I collected my books and went to bed. I still regret to this hour that I did not sit with him and talk with him, to discover what else the Devil wanted to do." At the Wartburg he would get his chance.

With these frequent, unwelcome visitations Luther had developed strategies to drive the demon away, and he eagerly passed his techniques along to his followers.

"What do you say to the Devil when he comes to torment you?" he was asked.

"Nothing," he replied. "Neither speak to him nor answer him. Leave him alone, and he will go about his business."

But the cold shoulder did not always work. Luther would say that the appearances of the malevolent spirit were manageable, but the Devil was to be feared most when he went beyond annoyance, beyond temptation, and sought to undermine the Word of God itself. Luther cautioned against the tactic of the woman from Magdeburg, who bragged about putting the Devil to flight by "rattling his belly" and spitting in his face. "Don't try that," Luther advised, for "the Devil is not to be taken lightly. He's a presumptuous spirit and is not inclined to yield. We run a great risk when we attempt more with him than we can do."

More effective was song, for music is a gift from heaven, Luther said, and the Devil hates it. "Our songs and psalms sorely vex and grieve the Devil," Luther instructed his admirers, "whereas our passions and irritations, our complaining and whining, our 'Alas!' or 'Woe-is-me!' please him well, so that he laughs in his fist." But ultimately it was only the finger of God that overcame the Devil. When the Devil disturbed his sleep, Luther was given to shouting: "*Omnia subiecisti sub pedibus eius!*"—"He has put everything [including the Devil] under his feet" (a loose translation of Hebrews 2:8).

Ultimately, the only way to drive away the Devil was through faith in Christ, Luther avowed, by saying loudly, "I have been baptized. I am a Christian."

And if all else failed, the last resort was to present one's backside to the Devil and fart. Answer stink with stink. "Then he will stop."

And thus for Luther, to live the devout life was to engage in a constant, intense, and profoundly important contest within oneself between God and the Devil. All Christians were subject to the temptations and strategies of Satan. To be aware of his presence and to have strategies to dispatch him was essential. Satan was not only the prince of death—for in Hebrews 2:14, the Apostle Paul assigns that power to him—but he was also the author and introducer of all sin.

To make the Devil real, to give him a face and even a backside, gave meaning to Luther's faith. To believe in a palpable, insistent, ever-present evil lent intensity to his beliefs. To trivialize the Devil, to dismiss him as an outdated, almost humorous phantom was to reduce faith to a one-sided intellectual idea, lacking the emotional intensity and energy of belief. Without the Devil, faith was a philosophical abstraction.

"When we do not have the Devil tied to our neck," Luther said, "we are but sorry theologians."

Still, after he left the Wartburg and was comfortable in his nightly drinking sessions with his companions at his Wittenberg pub, Luther recommended a more pleasant way to dispatch the annoying intruder. "A good bumper of old wine is the best remedy for quieting the senses, procuring sleep, and escaping the Devil," he observed, no doubt to cheers and raised mugs. And when beer was the beverage of choice, he would raise his mug lustily and say, "A flagon of beer to despise the Devil with!"

THERE MAY BE NO MORE VIVID SYMBOL OF LUTHER'S SOJOURN at the Wartburg than the ink stain on the wall of his modest cell. It has remained there through the centuries, perhaps even refreshed every year by the custodians of the Luther legend for the visitors who come to ponder this most intense period of the Reformer's life.

The story of how the stain ended up on the wall is told in many different ways. Perhaps the best rendition has Luther actually wrestling with the Devil, no doubt in the guise of a stout and filthy papist, and throwing his inkwell at his opponent during a critical moment in the match. But more plausible is the Devil's turn as a fly. This entomological annoyance, Luther tells us, tormented him day and night, as he sat at his desk writing his essays and translating the Bible. Luther knew it was the Devil, because the insect liked to settle on the pristine, white pages of his Bible and leave a dirty stain, as if to say, "I have been here!" And that, Luther believed, was the Devil's modus operandi. He looked for a pure and innocent heart, settled on it, and corrupted it.

One night after Luther had finished his studies and had extinguished his candle, the Devil announced his presence by shaking a bag of nuts that had been given to the Reformer as a gift. "Get about your business!" Luther shouted at him, whereupon the bothersome fly appeared and started buzzing around Luther's ears. In anger Luther picked up his ink bottle and threw it at the fly, splattering the wall and creating the famous ink stain.

The Devil. By Albrecht Dürer.

Fifteen years after his banishment at the Wartburg, he sat down to remember—or perhaps to imagine—the one extended conclave he had with the Devil during his confinement. In this colloquy, Luther claimed, he and the Devil discussed important points of faith and religious practice. Ironically, the Reformer cast himself as weak and indecisive during the encounter, daunted by an aggressive and persuasive Devil. Luther adopted a polite, respectful, deferential posture toward the dark prince, the embodiment of the phrase about giving the Devil his due.

"Listen, learned doctor," the Devil began. "You know that for fifteen years you have said private Masses nearly every day. What if such Masses are a horrible idolatry? What if the body and blood of Jesus Christ is not present, and you are making others adore simply bread and wine and nothing else? "

"I am an ordained priest," Luther replied. "I have received unction and consecration from the hands of the bishop. I have done all that my superiors have commanded in the obedience I owe to them. Why should I not consecrate the bread and wine, since I am solemnly proclaiming the words of Jesus Christ himself?"

"All that is true," the Devil responded. "The Turks and Pagans also do everything in their temples through obedience to their superiors, and they perform all their ceremonies solemnly. The pagan priests of Jeroboam (1 Kings 12:31) also did everything with zeal and with their whole heart against the true priests at Jerusalem. What if your ordination and consecration is as false as the priests of the Turks and Samaritans, and if your worship is just as false and impious as theirs?"

And then the Devil proceeded with a personal attack on Luther and on the very core of Catholic belief, as Luther had been practicing it for fourteen years. He began with the charge that Luther was a false witness to Jesus Christ, that his celebration of the Eucharist was an impious, anti-Christian travesty. More pointedly, he sought to undermine Luther's consecration as a priest. At the very moment of his investiture, Luther had no real knowledge of Jesus Christ, the Devil asserted, regarding the Savior as a severe judge only. As such, the novitiate deprived Christ of his capacity for mercy and, with that, his glory. Luther was no different from the infidel Turks, the Devil scoffed. "Therefore you received unction and the tonsure and sacrificed at the mass as a Pagan not as a Christian."

Next, the Devil turned to the sacrament of the Eucharist itself, heaping contempt on the manner in which Luther and other priests celebrated private Masses alone, a Mass for its own sake and a sacrifice, as an exclusive, private act, not for the people broadly. It was, therefore, no "communion" at all, but a private vanity. "What sort of a priest are you anyway?" the Devil teased. "Weren't you ordained not for the Church but for yourself? You mumbled those words, 'Do this in memory of me . . .' between your teeth as if you were whistling. They were words for you alone. Is it for that, you unworthy and faithless monk, you were ordained?"

And so the sacraments were a sham. Why not, argued the Devil, have people baptize themselves without the false presence of an interloper? Why not let priests consecrate themselves—or lovers marry themselves—and the dying give themselves extreme unction?

Weakly, Luther replied that to refute the Devil he was using the weapons he had employed against the papacy: that he was abiding by the intention of the church in celebrating the Mass. To this the Devil shouted back at him violently, "Show me where it is written that a wicked unbeliever can stand at the altar of Jesus Christ and proclaim the sacrament of the Church? Oh, your audacity! You do these things in darkness. You wish to defend your abominations by invoking the intention of the Church. How can you know the intention of the Church? Wherefore, blasphemer, do you make use the name of Jesus Christ to cover your falsehood and impiety?"

In a final, contemptuous sally, the prince of darkness said to Luther, "You have not consecrated anything. You have only offered bread and wine like all the pagans. By a traffic infamous and insulting to God, you have sold your work to Christians, not as a servant of God and Jesus Christ, but only for your belly. Was ever such abomination heard in heaven or on earth?"

In the face of this violent assault, Luther seemed crestfallen, apologetic, and beaten. "It is true that the Devil is a liar," he said. "But he does not lie when he accuses us. He comes to combat with the twofold testimony of the law of God and our conscience. I cannot deny that I have sinned. I cannot deny that my sin is great. I cannot deny that I am guilty of death and damnation."

In this encounter, at least, Luther's diabolical foil seems to have won the day. The Devil had convinced him that the Mass was false and idolatrous. Preaching and simple faith had to replace the rituals of worship. To Philipp Melanchthon on August 1, 1521, he wrote, "I shall never say another private Mass in all eternity."

In a sense this colloquy with the dark prince at the Wartburg was meant to be Luther's ultimate identification with St. John the Evangelist. Just as St. John's visions in the Book of Revelation came during his solitude in Patmos, so Luther's revelations could only come from his seclusion. Just as the prophet St. John had been banished by the anti-Christian forces of the emperor Domitian, so the prophet Martin Luther had been banished by Domitian's successor, Charles V. Just as prophecy was suppressed as a political crime in the first century after Christ's death, so it was in Luther's time. Just as St. John's visions rattled the powers in Rome and yet lasted forever in a new, vivid faith, so would Luther's prophecies rattle the new Rome and lead to a renewal of the original faith.

So he believed, and so it happened.

Nine

THE NEW CREATURE

I T IS A WONDER THAT ONE SO OBSESSED AND FRENZIED AND driven as Luther would ever relax and take in the pleasures of his serene, sylvan existence. There is only one example of this during the furtive August period, a time when Luther disentangled himself from the Devil, put down his quill and ink, and allowed himself a moment free of reflection and self-mortification. It was a short-lived respite, but from this episode, at last, a picture emerges of Luther doing something other than scribbling at his simple writing table in his cloistered room, pondering great and profound questions of creation and faith and human nature. Instead, at least for a day or two, he acted like the knight-errant he was supposed to be.

His amiable, polite jailer, Hans von Berlepsch, was eager to promote the illusion of his inmate as a strapping political refugee. In mid-August, the captain persuaded Jonker Jörg to go out on a hunt. When they met people along the way, he was to stroke his beard as aristocrats do and keep his hand at the ready on the handle of his sword. Once underway, Luther's curiosity ran to the question of how men "with nothing to do" amused themselves

119

with such dalliances. He wanted to experience "the bittersweet pleasures of heroes."

To Spalatin a few days later he described both the joy and the pity of his romp in the countryside. The heroic hunters bagged two hares and felled a few partridges, but Luther surmised that it would be more sport and a fairer contest to go after real game like bears and wolves, big game that could stoutly defend themselves rather than become innocent prey to men's snares and dogs. The hunting party had captured a little live rabbit and gave it to the faux knight, who promptly enfolded it lovingly in the sleeve of his cloak, only to have a vicious hound sniff it out, break through his cloak with its teeth, and kill it.

Characteristically, Luther found allegory in the rabbit's death. The bears, wolves, and foxes of his imagination were wicked teachers—inevitably, the bishops and theologians of Rome. They were the brood of the Devil, men who hunted defenseless creatures and innocent souls with their arsenal of deadly weapons. Hell would be their home. In paradise, Luther told Spalatin, the lovers of the hunt will be game for Christ, the best hunter of them all. Only He can catch and protect and save all the world's innocent creatures, like the little rabbit in his cloak.

"I'm sick of this kind of hunting," he wrote plaintively.

BY AUGUST OF 1521, LUTHER HAD LONG SINCE LEFT THE safe arena of polite academic discourse with its emphasis on precise argument and had embraced passionate ad hominem demaguery. He had surrendered himself, said his detractors, to "an invective of dazzling rhetoric." With eloquent advocacy and frenzied anger he had, publicly at least, discarded all critical reasoning. He was speaking to the masses now, and he had cut himself adrift from his Catholic moorings entirely. "The Gospel," he wrote at one point, "cannot be introduced without tumult, scandal and rebellion." And at another: "The Word of God is a sword, a war, a destruction, a scandal, a ruin, a poison." Catholic bishops, cardinals, and priests should be attacked "with every sort of weapon, and we will wash our hands in their blood."

By this time, of course, he was totally unapologetic about his invective and oblivious to criticism. He would no longer allow his detractors "the honor" of judging his teaching. "I shall not be judged by any man, not even by any angel," he wrote. But he reserved the right to judge the doctrine of the church. For his contemptuous disobedience, the church might try to take his life, but "you will annihilate neither my name nor my teaching. . . . If I live, you shall have no peace from me, and if you kill me, you shall have ten times less peace."

If the church insisted on portraying him as a wild boar, so be it. He would embrace it. He invoked the passage in the Old Testament Book of Hosea: "I will meet them as a bear that is bereaved of her cubs, and will rip the membrane of their heart. I will devour them like a lion" (13:8). And so it was with him. With the allegory of the hunter and the hunted fresh in his mind from his ride in the countryside, he remarked, "I shall be, as Hosea says, a bear on the road and a lion in the street."

As his incandescent revolutionary power became more and more evident over the course of his time at the Wartburg, his critics said that his goal was nothing less than to pull down the entire edifice of the Roman Catholic Church. Luther responded to this accusation in a tract he published in both Latin and German, entitled *Against the Falsely Called Spiritual State of the Pope and His Bishops*: "They say, 'There is fear that a rebellion may arise against the spiritual Estate.' I reply: 'Is it just that souls are slaughtered eternally, that these blockheads may disport themselves quietly? It is better that all bishops should be murdered, and all religious foundations and monasteries razed to the ground, than that one soul should perish, not to speak of all the souls ruined by these dummies.' What good are they except to live in lust from the sweat and labor of others and to impede the word of God?"

After it was finally published in 1522, the church responded that "his vocabulary of vituperation attains a height exceeded only by himself."

The tract put on display the public Luther: the provocative, abrasive, coarse, uncompromising revolutionary who attacked any critic or authority who dared to challenge him. But in his monk's cell his main focus remained his scholarship and his teaching. In early August he had again taken up his original intention, defined as he had arrived at the Wartburg in May: to focus on Advent and Christmas by translating from the Latin his existing seasonal homilies, and perhaps to write new sermons. His overall plan was to have his sermons ready for the four Advent Sundays—Christmas Day, the feast of St. Stephen (the first Christian martyr) on December 26, the feast of St. John the Apostle (the author of the fourth Gospel) on December 27, New Year's Day, and Epiphany. This would further his effort to explain biblical texts in the parlance of the German street.

But the project came in fits and starts.

In June he had finished his Christmas eve homily, whose text was Paul's Letter to Titus: "We should live soberly, righteously, and godly, in this present world; Looking for that blessed hope, and the glorious appearing of the great God and our Saviour Jesus Christ; Who gave himself for us, that he might redeem us from all iniquity, and purify unto himself a peculiar people, zealous of good works" (2:12–14). On June 10 he sent this sermon off for printing, but then put the wider project aside until he came back to it in August.

Although he couldn't have known it at the time, his focus on translating extracts of the Gospels from Latin into vernacular

German was setting the stage for his magnum opus. In November he had finished the Christmas homilies and sent them off for publication. But the Advent homilies, though they were supposed to come first, would not be ready until well into the new year.

This work on Christmas became known as the Wartburg Postil. The word "postil" derives from the Latin phrase *post illa verbe*, "after the word of Scripture." The first postils were produced by the order of Charlemagne in the ninth century, but Luther's postils were to become the most famous ever written. Through his postils the engine of translation was cranked up and running smoothly.

As fall approached, he was again in great physical pain. September 9, 1521, was an especially bad day. For six days he had suffered from a gradual worsening of his gastrointestinal agony. His hemorrhoidal lesions were raging. "I am miserable and growing sluggish and languid and cold in spirit," he wrote to George Spalatin. "Today I had an elimination of such difficulty that I almost passed out. Now I sit aching as if in labor confinement, wounded and sore, and shall have little rest this night. . . . I would have healed from all soreness if the elimination had moved more easily. But whatever heals in four days is wounded again by elimination." He took this as another sign that the Devil was tormenting him and the Lord was testing him. "I write this not for any sympathy but that you may congratulate me, praying that I may be worthy to become fervent in Spirit."

On the same day, in a letter to Melanchthon, Luther questioned his clerical status in the light of papal and imperial disfavor. Was he still a doctor of Holy Scripture, or was he no longer even entitled to call himself an ecclesiastic? Were his vows null and void? Was he really the "wild boar" that Leo X's excommunication bull had labeled him? "Am I free and no longer a monk?" he asked. At the loss of his official standing, he would say, wryly no doubt, "I am as shocked as an ass who has lost its bag."

In his letters to Melanchthon, Spalatin, and Amsdorf on this day, he projected from the tainted status of his own vows to philosophize about what he called the "slavery of vows." If a vow is impossible to keep, he wondered, did that make the vow itself invalid or, worse, a sacrilegious act of hypocrisy? If, for example, a married couple cannot get along, does that nullify the marriage vow itself and make divorce both acceptable and necessary? Or more pointedly, if a monk cannot fulfill his vow of celibacy, did that make the vow invalid?

And then he got personal. He reminded Melanchthon of Hans Luther's anger when years ago the young Martin had secretly taken his monastic vow after the terrible thunderstorm: his father had wondered if his rash decision was not a delusion inspired by the Devil. That comment had stung Luther deeply, and he remembered it always. It gave him, he acknowledged, a "fierce and troubled conscience."

Questioning the validity of vows had reverberations in Wittenberg. Unrest was growing among the Augustinians, and the debate between them and the university professors like Karlstadt and Melanchthon had become fierce. In July Luther had proclaimed private Masses, said for money, to be idolatry, and in early October, led by Gabriel Zwilling, thirty-nine of forty Augustinians formally declared their refusal to say a private Mass. Zwilling dubbed it a "Devilish institution," and another Luther intimate and expert in canon law, Justus Jonas, proclaimed Masses for the dead to be sacrilegious for the soul. In July Karlstadt had proclaimed that celebrating Mass with only the bread of life and not the wine was a sin. Luther originally disagreed, not wanting yet to go that far. The laity, he felt, were the victims not the perpetrators in the denial of the chalice.

In early October Zwilling attacked the concept of venerating the consecrated host, and he came dangerously close to denying

Christ's presence in the bread and wine. At about the same time, a visiting delegation of the Order of St. Anthony visited Wittenberg and put on display their vows of obedience, chastity, silence, prayer, poverty, and manual labor as an emulation of Christ as a carpenter. With Zwilling leading the pack, the Antonian brothers were harassed and insulted. Melanchthon and Karlstadt, though they were in philosophical agreement with the Augustinian friars on the misuse of the Mass, tried to temper the furor and keep it on the level of amiable intellectual discourse—with mixed results.

Elector Frederick watched this growing unrest with concern and took action to slow down the revolution by issuing an order against the innovations in the Mass. But his demand was ignored. In the second week of November, thirteen friars threw off their cowls and fled the monastery. Zwilling chided and ridiculed the malingerers, and soon more followed.

From his remove at the Wartburg Luther viewed the fast-moving developments with dismay. He worried that friars were abandoning their vows without sufficient cause and that later this would implant a troubled conscience in them as well. Writing to his Augustinian brothers on November 1, he stressed that their movement was about the renewal of the church, not about its destruction or abandonment. He was still committed to reform from within. A Mass could still be said so long as it was said properly, in the evangelical way. He invoked again his concept of a universal priesthood with no hierarchy, using as his reference Romans 12:1–3: "I beseech you brethren to present your bodies as a living sacrifice, holy and acceptable to God. Be not conformed to this world, but transform yourself by renewing your mind. . . . For I say to every man do not think of yourself more highly than you ought to think."

On November 22, he reaffirmed his concern in a letter to Spalatin. Of the friars who had discarded their cowls, Luther wrote, "they might have done this with a conscience not sufficiently strong." He hoped they would have "more confidence in themselves. It is certain that the monastic vow must be condemned now, if only for this one reason: the Word of God is not treated in the monasteries. Only unadulterated human lies rule there."

Meanwhile, Luther learned that there had been another brazen instance of the sale of indulgences. It had again been authorized by the archbishop of Mainz, Albrecht, in the Saxon town of Halle. Not only was Albrecht back in the indulgence game, but he had also come up with another ingenious ploy to raise money. The sinner could now pay to idolize the archbishop's sensational collection of relics, and with the visit the penitent could gain further credit against his days in purgatory. Later, Luther would make fun of this scheme by suggesting a few new relics that might help the good archbishop raise a little cash: three flames from the burning bush on Mt. Sinai, a few bristles of Beelzebub's beard, two feathers and an egg from the Holy Spirit, one half of the archangel Gabriel's wing, thirty blasts from the trumpets on Mt. Sinai, five strings from the harp of David, and a whole pound of the wind that roared by Elijah in the cave on Mt. Horeb.

But the new round of indulgences at Halle was no laughing matter, and Luther was furious. Characteristically, he dashed off a condemnation in white heat. Soon enough he learned that this and several other of his incendiary tracts had not been published. He had sent these tracts about the abuses of the Mass and the celibacy of monks to Spalatin but had heard nothing about their printing. The reason for the delay, as he was soon to find out, was that Elector Frederick had forbade their publication, not wanting Luther's ravings to stir things up further.

Not knowing this, Luther protested to Spalatin on November 12: "I will not endure such prohibition. I would rather lose you, and the prince, and all. For if I have withstood the archbishop's creature, the pope, why should I give way to this creature? It is all very well to talk about not disturbing the public peace, but will you endure the eternal peace of God to be disturbed by these impious works of perdition? You must not be moved by our bad repute among moderate men, for you know that Christ and His Apostles did not please men. We are not accused of wrong-doing, but only of despising impiety. The Gospel will not be overthrown if some of our party sin against moderation."

In those weeks of November the inmate continued to write frantically, as if his end was near. He penned a tract *On Monastic Vows* and dedicated it to his father. (Hans Luther was now sixty-two years old and living in Mansfeld.) The dedication contained some of the most poignant words Luther ever wrote, for he was writing to a father from whom, over his decision to become a monk, he had become estranged but with whom he had now reconciled.

He revisited the circumstances of that decision sixteen years earlier. It had been made in the grip of fear, spontaneously in the midst of a terrible thunderstorm in Stotternheim, and he had known it to be without his father's knowledge and against his will. He recalled what his father had said: "Let's hope that this is not a delusion derived from Satan." That remark went to the depths of his soul, Luther wrote now, as did another remark of his father back then, "Have you not heard that parents are to be obeyed?"

Now Luther suddenly proclaimed that his decision to become a monk had been wicked. It was a sin against his father's authority, and neither free nor voluntary. It was taken out of terror and superstition as a hot youth. As a result he had become a prime target for Satan. Given Satan's persistent effort to destroy or hinder him, he sometimes wondered "whether I was the only man in the whole world whom he was seeking."

Luther as Hercules. By Hans Holbein the Younger.

In retrospect, he asked himself now: Would his father still take him out of the monastery? Actually, his Lord had done his father's will. "He has taken me out Himself. What difference does it make whether I retain or lay aside the cowl and the tonsure?" he asked. His conscience had been freed, he proclaimed. It was a complete liberation. "I am still a monk and yet not a monk. I am a new creature, not of the pope but of Christ."

I
N THE FALL AND EARLY WINTER OF 1521 THE BLACK PLAGUE
revisited Wittenberg and large sections of Saxony. The cause
of the pestilence was laid vaguely to evil spirits or to the filth
in the streets or to poisonous vapors or to the Devil himself. (It
would not be definitively tied to infected rats and fleas until the
nineteenth century.)

In his salubrious remove at the Wartburg Luther received the
news of the epidemic with high alarm. The effects of bubonic
plague were horrible: it attacked the lymph nodes, producing
grotesque swelling under the arms and in the groin area, and led
to vomiting, shivering, shortness of breath, and high tempera-
tures before death. Though he did not describe the disease, no
doubt he could imagine the streets of his beloved town strewn
with bloated bodies, some of them belonging to his friends. And
while some of the afflicted were afraid to venture out, their bodies were found later in their houses, discovered only from the
stench.

With Luther's fertile imagination he worried especially about
the health of his beloved Philipp Melanchthon, the guardian of
his fragile movement. "I implore you not to let Philipp stay in
Wittenberg, if the plague breaks out there," he wrote to Spalatin
on October 7. "That head must be preserved so that the Word
which the Lord has entrusted to him for the salvation of souls,
may not perish." Despite the concern for him, Melanchthon
stayed, even after Elector Frederick ordered the evacuation of the
university on November 20.

But many fled Wittenberg, as they had done during another
visitation of the fatal illness in 1505, while others fell on their
knees in supplication to two saints, St. Sebastian from the third
century and St. Roch from the fourteenth century, who were
supposed to offer protection from the pestilence. During the
1505 epidemic Lucas Cranach had fashioned a plague painting

called *A Christian Heart* that featured the two saints kneeling before a swath of Wittenberg's spires.

Four years later, Luther would formally address the question of whether it was morally appropriate for a Christian to flee the plague. Those who were strong in their faith would stay, he argued, invoking Mark 16:18 about the faithful who could drink poison and not suffer, and Christ's command in John 10:11: "A good shepherd lays down his life for the sheep, but the hireling sees the wolves coming and flees." Those who had official positions, those who had care of the sick or the needy or the orphaned, those who had obligations to their neighbors: they were obliged to remain. But if one was not under any such obligations, fleeing was not wrong per se. Indeed, he wrote, it was appropriate to preserve life and avoid death if it could be done without harm to one's neighbor. One should take whatever medicines or other protections were available. Otherwise, exposing oneself rashly was a form of suicide. Therefore, those who flee should not be condemned.

"What else is the epidemic but a fire which instead of consuming wood and straw devours life and body?" he asked.

Luther reserved his greatest contempt for any infected person who neglected to take care not to infect others, or worse, who knowingly exposed others out of sheer wickedness or the fantasy of thinking the disease might gravitate from himself to those he infected.

"If any such persons are discovered," he wrote, "the judge should take them by the ear and turn them over to Master Jack, the hangman, as outright and deliberate murderers."

Ten

A CLANDESTINE
MISSION

IN LATE NOVEMBER LUTHER DECIDED THAT HE NEEDED TO SEE the volatile situation in Wittenberg for himself, and for good reason. In early December, a mob of students and townspeople in Erfurt interrupted a Mass in the city church, drove the priests from the altar, and seized all the missals. The next day forty students, described as "unrestrained and ignorant Martinians," stormed the Franciscan monastery, demolished the altars, and smashed the windows of the order's canon, as the civil authorities stood by and did nothing. Informed of this unrest, Elector Frederick took action to calm things down.

On December 5, 1521, Luther slipped out of the Wartburg and headed for Wittenberg. Accompanied only by a manservant, he traveled first to Leipzig, stayed overnight in an inn, and proceeded to Wittenberg and the home of his staunch supporter, Nicholas von Amsdorf.

Fifty-nine miles southwest of Berlin, Wittenberg at this time was the capital of the tiny Prussian duchy of Saxe-Wittenberg.

Wittenberg's Castle church at the time of the
95 Theses. CREDIT: STIFTUNG LUTHERGEDENKSTÄTTEN
IN SACHSEN-ANHALT, WITTENBERG

The town featured narrow cobblestone streets and half-timbered
houses. Its chief landmarks were the Elster Gate, where Luther
had burned his excommunication document; the town church
of St. Mary with its twin towers, built in 1281; and the Imperial Church or *Schlosskirche*, with its grand tower soaring over
the town, its baptismal font by Hermann Vischer decorated with
figures of the apostles, and a magnificent painting by Cranach,

depicting the Lord's Supper, baptism, and confession, over the altar. At the turn of the century Wittenberg had had a population of about 2,300 citizens, but in the previous few years, the number had doubled with the influx of students from all over Germany who wished to study at the feet of the great Reformer.

Predictably, town-and-gown tensions developed as the town grew. In the academic year of 1520–1521, things got out of hand as brawls broke out between the two factions. Students bridled at the ban on daggers, which was strictly enforced, and complained that they were constantly bullied and harassed by the locals. The journeymen artists in Lucas Cranach's bustling studio came in for special condemnation, for it was well known that they carried weapons beneath their smocks, probably with Cranach's sufferance. Before he left for the Diet of Worms, Luther was forced to take sides and preached from the pulpit of the parish church against unruly students.

In his first few days home incognito, Luther reconnected warmly with his old friends, including Melanchthon and Cranach, and engaged in long colloquies about the movement and the state of affairs. During these seven furtive days in his hometown Cranach rendered a remarkable portrait of the Reformer as Knight George (see p. 92). The painting gives Luther a steady sidelong stare, startling clear eyes, and an athletic build. His hair is curly and full, though closely cropped, and his fulsome facial hair cascades down into copious muttonchop whiskers and handlebar mustache. His face remains thin, and his eyes are intense, as if he feels uncomfortable in his disguise. This was not a man to be trifled with.

When the painting was finally done in early 1522, Cranach appended a few lines of Latin to its base:

> *Jesus is the one hope for me. He I will not deceive*
> *So long as I have Him, farewell, dishonest Rome.*

On this visit home Luther wished to keep his presence in Wittenberg secret, avoiding the Augustinian monastery altogether so as "not to betray myself." He also kept his distance from the elector's court in order not to compromise his supporters there. Still, upon his arrival he immediately wrote a letter of annoyance to Spalatin about his unpublished work.

"I fear that the material might have been intercepted on the way or have been lost in some other way by the messenger," he began, as if to give Spalatin an out. "Nothing would disturb me more than to learn that these manuscripts had reached you and that you were holding them back. I have dealt in these little books with themes of the greatest urgency. If you have them, for goodness sake, curb your moderation, for you accomplish nothing by rowing against the stream. What I have written I want published, if not in Wittenberg, then somewhere else." He ended this blast with a warning: "Whoever destroys lifeless paper will not quench the spirit. If the manuscripts have been lost or if you have kept them back, I will be so embittered that I will write more vehemently on these points than ever."

As Elector Frederick's secretary, Spalatin was too close a friend and too important a supporter for Luther to berate him too harshly, lest he alienate his most important protector, the elector himself. With disturbances breaking out all over, the elector had a complicated political problem that Luther would soon come to appreciate. And so in the final paragraph of his December 5 letter, he softened. "Everything I hear and see pleases me very much," he wrote. "May the Lord strengthen the spirit of those who want to do right."

Despite his disagreements with Andreas Karlstadt and his worries about things getting out of control, he seemed to acquiesce in the principal reforms that had moved forward in his absence and under Karlstadt's tutelage. The chalice was now being offered to the laity at Mass, private Masses had been eliminated, icons were removed from churches, Augustinians were leaving the order in droves, and even Karlstadt's incendiary views about celibacy and monastic vows had been well received. Hearing the details in Amsdorf's living room, Luther was mollified—at least temporarily.

Nevertheless, he mentioned to Spalatin his dismay about "rumors of improper conduct by some of our people." The latest violent disturbances at Erfurt had reached his ears by this point, and they were part of a pattern. Three weeks earlier he had learned about Wittenberg students rioting against a visiting delegation of the Hospital Brothers of St. Anthony. Luther viewed this behavior as reprehensible. When he returned to "my wilderness," he wrote to Spalatin, he intended to write a stern warning against such violence. He kept his promise. Indeed, he did not wait to return to the Wartburg and penned his "sincere admonition" to all Christians, against insurrection and rebellion, while he was still in Wittenberg.

His message was that rebellion—especially violent rebellion—was not the straight path to reformation. While he sympathized with the just aspirations of the common person against tyranny and oppression, he insisted that justice could, and should, be obtained only through prayer, confession, and sincere argument. Employing force was the work of the Devil, he said, for it would only discredit the movement. As such, violent insurrection was forbidden by God, and protesters must be restrained and not encouraged to cross the line into violence. His writings and his name should not be used to validate such self-defeating disruptions.

The Reformer ended his *Sincere Admonition to All Christians to Guard Against Insurrection and Rebellion* on a personal note. His supporters must not call themselves Lutherans. "I ask that men make no reference to my name. Let them call themselves Christians, not Lutherans. What is Luther? The teaching is not mine. Neither was I crucified for anyone. How then should I, poor stinking maggot-fodder that I am, come to have men call the children of Christ by my wretched name?"

On December 12, at the end of his secret visit to Wittenberg and now fully apprised of the events in both the town church and the elector's court, Luther wrote again to Spalatin. The letter contained his characteristic balance of praise and reproach. As he bade a fond farewell to the elector's court, he could not restrain himself from suggesting that perhaps Frederick's secretary was both too sophisticated and too timid. Nevertheless, he agreed to allow Melanchthon to edit his tract against the indulgence at Halle, which included his attack on Cardinal Albrecht, and to delete its most incendiary passages. And he further agreed to permit its publication to be postponed. He could not, however, permit Albrecht's imprisonment of married priests to go unnoticed, even though some had now been released. Those released had been forced to renounce their marriages, which Luther could not abide: "You write that the Cardinal's officials have released them, as if this release is not seven times more cruel than captivity, since these poor men were forced to perjure themselves and deny the truth of God."

His confrontational letter to the archbishop of Mainz about the Halle indulgence had to be forwarded. In it he wrote, "Perhaps Your Elector Grace thinks I am now out of action and that you are safe from me, that this monk is well under the control of His Imperial Majesty, Charles V. But Your Grace should know that I shall do what Christian love requires, even the gates of hell not withstanding." He would not be silent over the archbishop's professed ignorance of the matter. Albrecht was robbing poor people, and his indulgences were nothing but fraud and knavery. Moreover, the archbishop must immediately cease his harassment of priests who married "to avoid un-chastity." Marriage was their "God-given right."

Then he issued an ultimatum: If the indulgence campaign was not stopped, he would feel duty-bound to attack Albrecht publicly, to show the difference "between a bishop and a wolf."

"I have admonished Your Grace enough," Luther wrote. "According to St. Paul's teaching, it is the time to accuse, ridicule, and punish publicly all the obvious offenders, so that the cause of the offense may be driven out of God's kingdom." The inspiration for this phrase came from Paul's First Epistle to the Corinthians: "God judges those who are outside. Remove the wicked man from among yourselves" (5:13).

He gave the archbishop fourteen days to respond to his letter positively. If no answer was received, he would publish his incandescent condemnation of Albrecht.

BESIDES THE PLEASURE OF SEEING OLD FRIENDS, PRODDING THE Elector's court, and judging the movement's state of affairs, Luther's chief reason for the secret Wittenberg trip was to discuss a translation of the Bible. The subject had been under discussion with Melanchthon for over a year.

The standard Bible in use at the time was the old and perplexing Vulgate, originally translated into Latin from Greek and Hebrew texts by St. Jerome in the fourth century and officially authorized by the Roman Catholic Church for over a thousand years. Over the centuries monks had copied the Vulgate in remote monasteries throughout Europe. Numerous errors had crept into the text as a result of this disparate copying, and marginal notes had been added, making its rendering tedious and unwieldy. Few outside the clergy could read its Latin. The Gutenberg Bible of 1455 was the Vulgate, and its cost was astronomical: the equivalent of two hundred cows or a large house.

The first printed German translation of the Vulgate had appeared in 1466 in Strasbourg and was based upon a handwritten German translation from the fourteenth century. By the time of Luther's birth, eight more translations had been printed, and by 1521 eighteen anonymous translations were in existence.

But these Bibles were very expensive and therefore were owned only by the rich. With each translation from the Vulgate, the Holy Scripture became even more inaccessible and its language more convoluted. Additionally, the hierarchy of the church opposed translation into the local language, thinking that it weakened the authority of bishops.

Moreover, there was no such thing as standard German. Dialects proliferated throughout the land, to the extent that one dialect was totally incomprehensible to another. In Luther's own household his mother spoke the low German of Thuringia, while his father spoke the high German of Saxony-Anhalt. At times these two dialects were unintelligible to one another.

For several years before Luther fled to the Wartburg, he had devoted himself to translating and explaining Scripture in the language of the people. Since 1517 he had translated important passages of the New Testament, especially from the Gospel of St. Matthew, at times experimenting with the wording of the Vulgate and at other times going back to earlier Greek texts. In the preceding months he had written on the Anti-Christ, on the Thirty-Sixth and Sixty-Seventh Psalms, on the Epistles and the Gospels, and on the Magnificat of Mary. These, along with his political tracts, might now seem to him as trial runs for his most important effort of all.

"All this is in German," he was to say of this preliminary work. "I am born for my Germans. It is they I wish to serve."

In Wittenberg it was decided that he would harness himself to his translation and extend his stay in his Patmos until the following Easter. He would undertake the work alone and concentrate exclusively on the New Testament, the shorter book. While his mastery of Greek was total, his grasp of ancient Hebrew was elementary. To confront the daunting task of the Old Testament, he would need the hands-on help of his colleagues in Wittenberg. And so the Old Testament could be put off to a later time.

At the Wartburg he had a copy of the Greek version of the New Testament called the *Textus Receptus* or "received text," which the great humanist Erasmus had published in 1516 and revised in 1519. Erasmus had translated from six classic Greek texts that did not encompass the whole of the New Testament. (He translated the missing parts directly from the Latin Vulgate.) Luther admired Erasmus's scholarship and literary skill, though not his humanistic theology. With the Latin translation printed side by side with the Greek, the *Textus Receptus* became Luther's primary source, while ancient Hebrew texts served as a backup. Beyond these texts, he had in his own head a vast compilation of random translations he had made over the previous years.

Immediately upon his return to the Wartburg, he got to work.

Eleven

TWENTY-SEVEN BOOKS
IN TEN WEEKS

O NE CAN ONLY IMAGINE THE SPARE LOOK OF LUTHER'S CELL as he settled into his monumental task of translating the New Testament. With only his Greek and Hebrew texts as physical references, and no library to consult or clutter, delay or confuse his labor, his concentration was total. It would be easy to romanticize the process. But a more realistic vision involves sweat and frustration, long hours, and a feeling of being overwhelmed. He approached the assignment with awe. Later, he would call it "a great and worthy undertaking" and say that, given the unsatisfactory Bibles then available to the common person, "the people require it." But the language of the Bible dazzled him. He truly believed that he was dealing with the very words of God.

"One should tremble before each letter of the Bible, more than before the whole world!" he would say later. "God is in every syllable. No iota is in vain."

His first challenge was to establish the rules for his translation. Above all, he needed to keep his audience upmost in his mind.

What could a typical German understand? What should be the tone? What should be the grammar? "It is not enough to know the grammar of a biblical passage," he would say later. "One must observe the sense. I held fast to the meaning . . . as if I understood neither Greek nor Hebrew nor Latin."

In his first days of labor, he evolved two basic principles of translation. The first was to reduce all things to the most general, basic origin and type. "If a passage is obscure I consider whether it treats of grace or of law, whether wrath or forgiveness of sin, and with which of these it agrees better. By this procedure I understand the most obscure passages." The second was to submit ambiguous passages to the original Hebrew and not lazily fall back on literal translation, as he felt the Talmudic scholars had done. "The Jews go astray so often in the Scriptures because they do not know the true contents of the books. If one knows the contents, the sense must be chosen that is nearest to it." For the common reader, the goal was "to make Moses so German that no one would suspect he was a Jew."

In whose language was this to be written? Should his tone be lofty and correct, like the learned speech of the royal courts of the Holy Roman Empire in Vienna or the official language of the Electorate of Saxony? Or should it be conversational, the tongue of the street? If so, which street? At this time there were seventeen ways to write German in Wittenberg. Which of these should he choose or what combination?

Soon enough he made his choice.

"You've got to go out and ask the mother in her house, the children in the street, the ordinary man in the market," he explained later. "Watch their mouths move when they talk, and translate that way. Then they'll understand you and realize you are speaking German to them."

As Luther began his work, he knew that the eventual product would be highly controversial. In his mind was the proverb "He

Luther as St. Jerome. Credit: Stiftung Luther-
Gedenkstätten in Sachsen-Anhalt, Wittenberg

who builds along the road has many masters." In his boldness he
saw himself as the successor of St. Jerome, the first translator of
the Bible. The fourth-century saint also had many masters—and
critics. St. Jerome, too, was berated as incompetent by "people
who were not worthy to clean his boots," Luther knew. When
Jerome himself had been asked by Pope Damasus to translate the
ancient Latin Scriptures, he tried to get out of the assignment.

"Is there anyone learned or unlearned," St. Jerome had wondered, "who, when he takes the volume in his hands and per-
ceives that what he reads, does not suit his settled tastes, will not
break out immediately into violent language and call me a forger
and profane person for having the audacity to add anything to the

ancient books, or to make any changes or corrections in them?" But Jerome had scoffed at his critics, calling them "two-legged asses" and "yelping dogs."

Luther, inevitably, was more coarse. His detractors would criticize, but then they would use his translation as theirs. They would stick to his work "like shit to a wagon wheel." A violent reaction was inevitable. The world will criticize, he was to say. That was the way of the world.

Within a day of setting to work, he jump-started his process with the first twelve verses of Matthew: the birth of Christ, the treachery of Herod, the journey of the wise men to Judea guided by a star in heaven. Luther had translated these verses in the latter part of November, before his secret trip to Wittenberg, as he wrote his Christmas sermon called "The Christmas Postil."

But after those twelve verses he was in new territory. In times past he had relied on the Latin of the Vulgate. Now he saw the literal Latin as a confusing and meaningless obstacle to speaking good German. Glancing ahead, the insufficiency of Latin became dramatically clear. In Luke 1:28, for example, when in the Vulgate the angel greets the Virgin Mary with the salutation "Hail Mary, full of grace . . . ," Luther balked. What good German would say such a thing? he asked himself. What did it mean to say "full of grace?" Was it like a keg full of beer or a purse full of money? he asked himself. Luther translated the salutation simply as "God greet you, dear Mary." That is all the angel meant to say, he felt.

With Matthew 12:34, he had a similar issue. There, the phrase in the Vulgate was "*Ex abundantia enim cordis os loquitur*," whose literal translation is "Out of the excessiveness of the heart the mouth speaks." Is that speaking German? What is "excessiveness of the heart" anyway? Is it like the excessiveness of a house or of a stove or of a bench? The common man of the German street or the German mother in her house would say, "What fills the heart overflows the mouth." Now that was speaking good German.

Another hurdle presented itself in the story about Mary Magdalene in Matthew 26 and Mark 14. There Mary Magdalene comes to Jesus in the home of Simon the leper as the high priests and scribes and elders are meeting in the palace of the high priest in Calaphas about seizing Jesus and killing him. She brings an alabaster box containing precious oil, and while Jesus is dining, she pours the oil over his head. The disciples are shocked, especially Judas, and ask, in the Vulgate, "Why has the loss of ointment occurred?" What kind of German is this?, Luther scoffed. The German might think the ointment was lost and should be looked for and found. But the true German would say, "What's the reason for this waste?" or "Why this extravagance?" or "What a shame about the oil!"

From the beginning he determined to translate not literally but rather freely, relying on his insight into the essential meaning of the verse, and being spare, direct, and vigorous in his rendering. When it came to words like "joy," "love," and "heart," he would stress their relation to faith in God. In Matthew 11:28— "Come unto me all ye that labor and are heavy laden, and I will give you rest"—he substituted the word "labor" with "toil" to stress the empathy of Jesus for the common worker.

And yet the dialects of the vernacular German had their own deficiencies, and so it was not so easy to choose the lingo of "the person in the street." Which street and which person? Translating Hebrew phrases into common German, he said, was like teaching a nightingale how to crow like a rooster. The word for "boat," for example, was commonly *Kahn*, but also *Kleinschiff*, *Nachen*, and *Weidlung*. Which to use? And homonyms often had different spellings: *Rad* or *Rat*; *fiel* or *viel*. Conversely, while Hebrew had twelve different ways to say the word "God" German had only one way.

Draft page of Luther's translation. CREDIT: FORSCHUNGSBIBLIOTHEK, GOTHA

When one compares the complexity, speed, and intent of Luther's translation not only to the Vulgate but also to the King James Version of the Bible ninety years later, Luther's translation is even more impressive. If Luther's fundamental approach was to make the Bible accessible to the common person, the approach of King James's translators was to please and glorify the king himself with elegant, poetic verse. Their process in the early 1600s would take ten years, not ten weeks, and there were forty-eight translators, not one.

The difference in the two approaches can be seen in some comparative examples, along with certain passages that must have appealed directly to Luther's desperate situation.

For Matthew 5:15, the Vulgate reads: "Neither do men light a lamp and put it under the measure, but upon the lamp-stand, so as to give light to all in the house." And the King James Version reads: "Neither do men light a candle, and put it under a bushel, but on a candlestick; and it giveth light unto all that are in the house." Luther is more direct: "One does not light a lamp and put it under the bushel, but on the stand; and it shines everywhere in the house."

For Matthew 6:11, both the Vulgate and the King James read: "Give us this day our daily bread." Luther's version is more insistent: "Give us our daily bread today."

In the King James Version Matthew 6:34 reads: "Take therefore no thought for the morrow: for the morrow shall take thought for the things of itself. Sufficient unto the day is the evil thereof." The Vulgate is harsher: "Sufficient for the day is its own trouble." But Luther changed the sense entirely. Perhaps thinking of the recent pestilence in Wittenberg, his last line reads: "It is enough that each day has its own plague."

In Matthew 7:6 the Vulgate reads: "Do not give to dogs what is holy, neither cast your pearls before swine, or they will trample

Luther translates the New Testament. By Paul Thurmann.
CREDIT: ULRICH KNEISE, WARTBURG FOUNDATION

them under their feet and turn and tear you." The King James Version is essentially the same. But Luther is more graphic: "You should not give holy things to dogs, nor throw your pearls to sows, lest they trample them under their feet, and then turn and tear you to pieces."

With Luke 1:57, if he had been merely translating the Vulgate word for word, he would have read about the birth of John the Baptist: "Now Elizabeth's full time of being delivered was come, and she brought forth a son." The King James Version reads: "Now Elisabeth's full time came that she should be delivered; and she brought forth a son." Why mince words? Luther probably asked himself. From the Greek text, he went for the essence: "When it was time for Elizabeth to have her baby, she gave birth to a son."

When he got to the Gospel of John, worried as he was about what was going on with his friends in Wittenberg, or what might happen to them in his absence, or what might happen to him if he were seized, he would surely have related emotionally to John 15:12–13 when he translated the verse: "My commandment is this. Love each other as I have loved you. Greater love has no one than this: to lay one's life down for his friends."

THERE IS NO RECORD OF HOW LUTHER SPENT CHRISTMAS OF 1521 in his solitary confinement. His last two letters of that year to the outside world were written on December 18. One was to Wenceslas Link, who had been dean of the theological faculty at Wittenberg University a decade earlier and now was the vicar general of the Augustinian order. It had fallen to Link to deal with the mass exodus of friars from the order—a matter Luther viewed as "tumultuous" and unnecessary, even though he had provoked it. Two months later, in February 1522, Link was to convene a general meeting of the order in Wittenberg. There a resolution passed allowing all friars to leave the order if they chose, without penalty or consequence.

Luther had urged just such a compromise in his December missive: "You cannot hinder any who may want to leave the monastery. It would be best at your upcoming chapter meeting to make a public proclamation that freedom be given those who wish to leave, according to the example of Cyrus." This was a reference to King Cyrus the Great of Persia, who, according to Ezra 1:1–3, issued a proclamation allowing Jews to depart their kingdom for Jerusalem and there to rebuild the Temple.

On the same day Luther also wrote to another Augustinian, John Lang, who then presided over the chapter in Erfurt. "Physically, I am healthy and well cared for," Luther wrote, "but I am also thoroughly buffeted by sins and temptations. Pray for me. From the wilderness, Martin Luther."

And then he receded into silence.

In a sense Luther had been celebrating Christmas since the early summer, as he labored on his Advent and Christmas postils. These homilies were meant to be delivered before the large audiences to which he was accustomed, with halls of worship packed and parishioners hanging from the rafters. Now, as the days ticked toward Christmas Day in his monk's cell, he may well have imagined the reaction to his new material before his accustomed throng. But he could only imagine.

He viewed the incarnation of God as a gift far superior to all other works of creation. Glory to God, peace on earth, and good will toward men—this was the supreme song of worship, sung first by the angels and now by men and women through the ages. Singing was central to the joy. He would quote one tart-tongued preacher as saying that if Mary had had more than one child, "we'd have to scream ourselves to death!"

But for the Christmas of 1521 there would be only a congregation of one, the captain of the Wartburg, Hans von Berlepsch. Just the two of them gathered for an intimate dinner high above the lovely Thuringia countryside, and their conversation tended toward the same message about the Virgin Mary that Luther had crafted in his Christmas postil.

Her real name was Miriam, meaning bitter myrrh, and he viewed her as a simple girl of about fourteen from the lowest station of life. The angel Gabriel had already visited her, and she had been made pregnant by the Holy Spirit, even before she was married to Joseph. It was her deep faith, more than the "mere trifle" of the Virgin birth, that interested Luther the most. "Had she not believed, she could not have conceived," he had written earlier in the year. In his "Magnificat," completed in June, he dealt with Mary's visitation to her cousin, Elizabeth, who in a similar twist was miraculously pregnant at an advanced age. He also dealt with Mary's touching relationship with Joseph. He wrote about their journey from Nazareth to Bethlehem in the dead of winter, their rejection at the inn, the absence of a single helping hand. "Do not make of Mary a stone," Luther wrote. She suffered the frigid cold and the rejection and the humiliation as any human being in her situation would, indeed especially those in the lowest station in life.

For so convivial a figure, it's hard to imagine Luther keeping to himself during those joyous days about which he had thought so deeply. It was a boisterous time for song and feasting. By this time his minder was well aware of the eminent personage he had in his protective care, and they surely would have established a deep bond. Unless the captain was sour and soulless—there is no evidence of this—he would certainly have wanted to partake of Luther's wisdom about the season. What a privilege to spend Christmas alone with such a man!

On Christmas eve he and von Berlepsch might have prayed together by candlelight, the wind whistling outside, with Luther conveying the essence of his Christmas eve sermon to his protector in a personal way. It took as its lesson the words from the Epistle of Paul to Titus 2:11–14 about the grace of God appearing to all people, about living soberly and righteously as they await the appearance of Jesus Christ. "We must make a two-fold use of the Word of God," he had written in the summer, "as both bread and weapon, for feeding and resisting; in peace and war. With one hand we must build, improve, teach, and feed all Christendom; with the other, oppose the Devil, the heretics and the world. For where the pasture is not defended, the Devil will soon destroy it."

And then the glorious day itself, with angels proclaiming to simple shepherds—not to kings and high priests—tidings of great joy and a multitude of the heavenly host breaking into song. From their high perch at the Wartburg Luther and Berlepsch might have visualized shepherds in the rolling fields and hills around them, and then as night fell the star of Bethlehem guiding the wise men. "These Magi were not kings, but learned men in the art of nature," Luther had written. They were like philosophers in Greece or professors in universities, natural scientists from the East or from Arabia. Their modest standing seemed to be important to him.

And the nativity itself? the captain might have wondered. "The swaddling clothes signify the preaching of the Gospel," Luther had written. "The manger signifies the place where Christians come together to hear the word of God. The ox and the ass stand for us."

No doubt the captain would have put on a great Christmas feast the next day, fitting for his prominent guest and featuring the bounty of Thuringia. The first course was likely a soup laced with pork, carrots, leek, onions, garlic, and barley, eaten with bread. This would be followed by the main course, featuring grilled venison (only nobles were allowed to hunt deer in the forest) and perhaps grilled wild boar and roasted goose, accompanied by red cabbage spiced with juniper berry, cloves, and lard, and white cabbage spiced with caraway. There were probably side dishes of carp from the Hörsel River, mounds of famous Thuringian bratwurst, potato dumplings, and potato salad, all to be washed down with beer or mead drunk from a cow's horn and an ample supply of Luther's favorite wine from the Rhine River.

And when it was over, perhaps three hours later, Martin Luther might well have repeated the remark that every German student from the sixteenth century onward associates with him: *"Warum furzet und rülpset ihr nicht? Hat es euch nicht geschmecket?"* Or in the vernacular English translation: "Why aren't you farting and burping? Didn't it taste good?"

Twelve

ROME

So long as Pope Leo X lived, Martin Luther remained in mortal danger. The death penalty implicit in Leo's papal bull of excommunication was tied to the life of its author. As a result, the length of Luther's stay at the Wartburg was bound up with the health of this strange, complicated pope. As long as Leo was alive, there would be no slackening of pressure.

For all the propaganda about Leo's charm and generosity, Luther could have no illusion about the pope's capacity for brutal revenge when he was angered. This had been demonstrated five years earlier, in 1516, when a plot to assassinate the pontiff was uncovered. The chief conspirator of this nefarious plot was the cardinal from Siena, Alfonso Petrucci, who had been a pivotal supporter in Leo's election to the papacy and then was angered at Leo's lack of gratitude for his support. In addition, Petrucci was livid at the treatment of his brother, who had been banished from Rome rather than promoted to prominence in the Curia.

At first, Petrucci considered making an attempt on the pope's life himself. But when this proved impractical, he recruited a prominent physician, Batista da Vercelli, to accomplish the deed.

The plan was for the physician to apply poisonous bandages to the painful fistula from which the pope suffered. But Petrucci fell under suspicion when incriminating letters between him in Siena and his secretary in Rome were intercepted. The Vatican devised a ruse to lure the cardinal back to Rome. And safe conduct was provided to him and certified by the ambassador to the king of Spain. Once he presented himself to the pope, however, Petrucci was seized and hauled off to the dungeons of Castel Sant'Angelo. So much for papal safe conduct. The Spanish emissary protested loudly. The pope replied that safe conduct did not apply to papal assassins.

And then the harsh examination began. In his dungeon Cardinal Petrucci was strangled to death by a Muslim executioner, since it would not do for a Christian to execute a cardinal of the church. Rigorous examination was applied to the lesser suspects, and the full scope of the plot became clear. The punishments began with several Sienese conspirators being drawn and quartered. But this method was not sufficient for the guilty physician himself. Once Batista da Vercelli was turned over to secular authorities, his flesh was grappled with red hot pincers, before his body was dragged by horses through the streets and then hanged at the bridge of the Castel Sant'Angelo.

Meanwhile, a papal consistory was held in which the pope angrily confronted Petrucci's co-conspirators, among them a handful of cardinals. After they tearfully confessed on their knees, the pope pardoned them before they were dismissed—upon the proviso that they pay a fine of 20,000 ducats each. In the end the plot had been a profitable enterprise for the pope: the windfall was promptly applied to Leo's debts.

Leo's treatment of Cardinal Petrucci foreshadowed the swift justice that Luther might expect if he fell into the hands of the church. Yet he was fortunate in one respect. In the summer of

1521 the Luther case had receded into the background in Rome, as other pressing matters captured the pope's attention. With the Edict of Worms the Vatican convinced itself that it now had the remedy to snuff out the "Saxon scandals." On June 7, as Luther began to hit his stride at the Wartburg, a satisfied Leo conveyed the great news of the edict to his cardinals at a papal consistory. After the conclave the cardinals in a festive mood repaired to the Piazza Navona to burn Luther's picture and books.

Uppermost in the pope's mind now was the military situation in northern Italy. The contest between the France of Francis I and the Holy Roman Empire of Charles V was centered around Milan, and Leo X had no alternative but to choose sides. Notorious for his indecisiveness, his manner of decision-making was to hesitate and procrastinate and turn a matter over endlessly, weighing all the permutations. In playing France off against the Holy Roman Empire, it was said that he "steered with two compasses."

But when France attacked Milan, Leo's way was clear, and he announced an offensive alliance with Charles V. Again there was a discrepancy between Leo's public posture and private feelings. In public he said tartly, "The French are as unbearable as allies, as they are formidable as enemies." In announcing an agreement with Charles, he again invoked the image of the sun and the moon. The "two real heads of Christendom" were to unite "in purifying it from all error, in establishing a universal people, in fighting the infidel, and in introducing a better state of things throughout."

When Luther heard of the alliance between the divine and secular powers in September, he was indifferent to this unholy alliance of two parties that were combining to exterminate him and his movement. To Spalatin he wrote a wry response: "The plans of the Pope and Emperor are not yet fully developed. God leads both as they deserve, and where they should be led." He compared the coalition to the ancient Amorites in the Bible (Genesis 15:16), a troublesome tribe of gigantic peoples who destroyed themselves by their own evil. "I rejoice and wish the Emperor this same good fortune," he said, "but only because of God's hidden plans."

In its weakness the Vatican's only hope was to maintain a balance of power. Now France was allied with Venice in opposition to Charles and the Vatican. It would challenge Leo's skill as a diplomat and his famous penchant for double-dealing: How was he to support Charles without alienating Francis I too severely? His apologists would say this delicate balancing act made him a true statesman of the Renaissance.

If Luther could make sport of the pope's gluttony, he also had fun with the pontiff's indecisiveness. Years later, with friends at his favorite pub in Wittenberg, he would relate his fable of the pope inviting two philosophers to dinner. For the pope's pleasure the two were to debate the mortality or immortality of the soul. When the debate was over, the pope was to decide which philosopher was correct. To the philosopher who defended the immortality of the soul, the pope said, "You seem to be stating the facts. But your opponent's discourse creates a cheerful countenance." Luther's conclusion: epicureans always gravitate to the argument that suits the flesh over the argument that suits the mind and relies on the facts.

That Luther at this point could be wry and amused by Vatican follies reflected the lessening of pressure. From the standpoint of the Reformer and his movement, Leo's preoccupation with geopolitics rather than raging German heresy during the summer and fall of 1521 was a godsend. It gave Rome's opponents breathing room to grow and consolidate.

On November 19, an imperial force broke through the walls of Milan, captured the city, and drove the enemy out. The French fled across the Alps, and the episcopal sees of Parma and Piacenza were restored to imperial and papal control. Leo X received this happy news a few days later, at his villa in Magliana on the Tiber, southwest of Rome. There he was enjoying one of his remarkable hunts, which were of quite a different nature from the one little hunt through which Luther had suffered with his captain outside the Wartburg Castle.

Because he was immensely fat and half blind, the pontiff was carried to his blood orgy in a litter. The spectacle was conducted at the bottom of a ravine at a spot where minions drove stags and boar from the slopes with loud horns and bells. As the pope watched with his one good eye, the animals were butchered at his feet. Simultaneously, on a good day, papal falcons were let loose to go after soaring vultures overhead, and if the party was lucky, an eagle might happen by and join the fight, sending lesser birds plummeting to their deaths.

"What a glorious day!" the pope was apt to cry out. After so invigorating a day of sport, he would repair to an evening banquet. These feasts featured ribald theater and deafening music, and were famous for their abundance, with up to sixty-five courses. A plate of peacock tongues was sometimes on the menu, and occasionally a huge pie was served, from which an infant would spring to spout poetic greetings to the guests.

But on this late November evening, the exertions of the hunt together with his excitement over the wonderful news from the front tired Leo. Wanly, he greeted the Swiss soldiers below his window and watched a bonfire being prepared. Then his body shook with a chill. His doctors thought it was a simple cold. He was transported back to Rome, where he died so quickly—on December 1, only one week after he had taken ill—that there was no time to administer the last rites.

The eight-year pontificate of Leo X, prince of Florence, had commenced with extravagant hope. Erasmus had proclaimed the advent of a golden age. It was predicted that this scion of the great Medici family would be a man of peace, a lamb rather than a lion. His coronation had possessed a splendor never before seen in Rome, having the feel of a victory parade for a Roman conqueror. Fountains had spouted wine instead of water. Special archways with heroic inscriptions had been built for the magnificent procession of cardinals and soldiers. Delegations of the Orsini and Colonna families bespoke a mood of reconciliation. The emblem of the Medici family was everywhere. Doorways were festooned with expensive fabric. His way was strewn with flowers, and the new pope rode a massive white horse while his former adversaries, the dukes of Ferrara and Urbino, had walked ahead bearing the pontifical standard. Minions walked alongside Leo, holding a canopy of embroidered silk overhead so that he would not become overheated. At Castel Sant'Angelo a delegation of Jews pressed forward with a book of their laws, asking for a reconfirmation of their rights.

Leo had replied grandiloquently, "We confirm, but we do not assent."

Only days before his death, this pope who had dedicated himself so enthusiastically to enjoying the papacy that had been thrust on him was being extolled for his great contributions to the arts, for making Rome a center of culture and learning, for his patronage of Raphael and Michelangelo, for his charm and cheerful nature, for his gay pageants and lavish banquets, and for his passion in defending Christendom against the heretical Luther and the infidel Turks.

With his death the pent-up antipapal sentiment in Italy boiled to the surface. The late pope was ridiculed for his extravagance, his self-indulgence, and his vulgar ostentation that had driven the papacy to penury and turned the Vatican into a pagan bawdy house. A Roman wag wrote:

Without the Church's sacraments, Pope Leo died, I'm told.
How could he e'er receive again what he himself had sold?

The verdict on Leo's reign as pope was harsh. The contemporaneous writer Sigismondo Tizio wrote, "It was harmful to the Church that her Head should delight in plays, music, the chase and nonsense, instead of paying serious attention to the needs of his flock and mourning over their misfortunes."

So quick had been the death of the pope that foul play was immediately assumed. Leo X's last words advanced the rumor, since he cried out that he had been murdered. The cohorts of the French king in Rome immediately came under suspicion, as did other more ruthless, Machiavellian characters with deep grievances, like the dukes of Urbino and Ferrara.

But the prime suspect was the pope's cup bearer, Bernabo Malaspina, who belonged to the French party and who had quickly and suspiciously fled Rome at the pope's death. It was remembered that immediately before the pope fell ill, Malaspina had given the pope a cup of wine, which Leo had spat out angrily and wondered aloud why he had been given so vile a potion to drink. The cupbearer was detained, but after inquiries, he was released. The cause of Leo's death was eventually determined to be malaria.

Since the Roman treasury was depleted from the pope spending six times what he was taking in from indulgences and other beneficences, the funeral arrangements were kept simple and cheap. An observer noted that the only candle that could be found to illuminate Leo's coffin was a stub of wax left over from the funeral of a cardinal a week before.

WITH THE NEWS OF POPE LEO X'S DEATH, HIS COUSIN AND chief adviser, Giulio de Medici, rushed back from the battlefield in Lombardy to Rome, confident of his accession to the tiara, and hopeful of realizing Leo's dream of Medici hegemony in Italy. Giulio's advantages were considerable. Given the penury of the Vatican treasury, he came as the candidate of Florence, with all that city's wealth and the wealth of the Medici. In this time of war he had military experience and was a Knight of Rhodes. He had considerable political experience as well. For the eight years of Leo's reign, Giulio had skillfully handled Vatican foreign policy as vice chancellor, while the pope amused himself in profane merriment.

Without question Giulio de Medici was cunning and talented, but the question lingered as to whether this Medici could be as competent as pope as he was as first prelate.

After the traditional Mass of the Holy Ghost, the doors of the Sistine Chapel were locked on December 27, 1521, and the papal conclave began. Great confusion and discord reigned among the thirty-nine cardinals who would vote, thirty-six of whom were Italian. Among these thirty-six were the candidates from the leading, wealthy dynasties of Renaissance Italy, including the Farnese, Colonna, Piccolomini, Orsini, and Pucci families.

The Medici scion entered the contest with the most votes, but he had stout competition. Henry VIII was vigorously promoting Cardinal Wolsey, offering 100,000 gold ducats for his election. The English king savored the possibility of Wolsey's election. "Like father and son we will dispense the power and the authority of the Apostolic seat, as though it is our own," Henry proclaimed, "and we will give law to the whole world." As the process unfolded, the English envoy wrote to Wolsey, "There is marvelous division here, and we were never likelier to have a schism." Wolsey even suggested to the king that he march troops on Rome to pressure the electors.

In time, Wolsey faded as a viable candidate, but opposition to Giulio remained strong. There was intense concern about one

Medici following another to the papal throne and thereby establishing a hereditary principle. His detractors emphasized that he was a bastard by birth, was a tyrant by inclination, and as a statesman had been complicit in the financial undoing of the Vatican. War between the forces of France and the Holy Roman Empire still raged in the north of Italy, pitting the imperialist faction against a French-Venetian faction in the Sacred College voting. Since Leo had sided with Charles V in the conflict, Francis I let it be known that if the cardinals elected another Medici, "who is the cause of this war, neither I nor any man in my kingdom will obey the Church of Rome." He was prepared to pay 1 million silver thalers upon the election of a candidate favorable to his side.

Days passed, with various Italian candidates rising and then fading, as the cardinals deliberated in isolation. The Sistine Chapel stank with foul air and smoke. After the fourth scrutiny of the leading candidates on January 4 produced no pope, the order was given to reduce the rations of the quarantined cardinals.

Since the Holy Spirit was believed to be quietly directing the proceedings, there was still a sense of optimism. The elegant ambassador for the Marquis of Mantua, Baldassare Castiglione, who was following the proceedings closely, wrote, "God will yet bring it to pass that the final result shall be better than anyone has dared to anticipate." With the tally stalled short of the needed two-thirds majority, it began to look as if the campaign of Giulio de Medici would fail. As more scrutinies were held without result, Castiglione wrote, "Every morning one awaits the descent of the Holy Spirit, but it seems to me that he has withdrawn from Rome."

With the cardinals in their confined cubicles, on reduced rations, and coughing from the stagnant air of the Sistine Chapel, the turning point finally came with the eleventh scrutiny on

January 9, 1521. The pivotal player was Cardinal Thomas Cajetan. He had been the papal legate in Germany from the onset of Luther's revolt and had examined Luther personally and effectively in 1518. Most significantly, Cajetan had also been responsible for drafting Luther's excommunication order for Leo X.

It is probable that Cardinal Cajetan was eager to move the Luther controversy back to the front of the electoral process, which until then had been dominated by war talk and political maneuvering. The way out of the current dilemma, he argued, was to tap a cardinal of good character outside the current list of contenders, one against whom nothing negative could be said and who as well would be a fierce opponent of Luther's insurgency. He knew just the man: a grand inquisitor who had worked closely with him in the campaign against Luther.

Cajetan's proposal smacked of an electioneering ploy to break out more votes for a leading candidate in a subsequent round. Blithely, the forces of the Medici candidate threw their support behind the measure in that dilatory spirit. With an eye to later rounds after this throwaway round, other blocs followed suit, and to the mortification of all, the dark horse was accidentally elected. At the cry of *"Papam Habemus!"* astonishment was universal.

The chance winner was a foreigner, a "German" rather than an Italian, and a "barbarian" to the Italians. Only once in recent centuries had a non-Italian been elected pope. That was a disaster named Alexander Borgia (Alexander VI), a Spaniard and the father of the bloodthirsty siblings of Caesare and Lucretia Borgia. Moreover, the new pope was said to be in the pocket of Charles V. One disgruntled cardinal remarked, "One might almost say that the Emperor is now Pope, and the Pope Emperor."

As the cardinals filed out of the Vatican, they were heckled. "Robbers! Betrayers of Christ's blood! Do you feel no sorrow in having surrendered the fair Vatican to German fury?" protesters shouted. One enterprising detractor posted a sign on the Vatican wall that read, "This palace to let." In Paris, Francis I scoffed at the new pope as a "creature" and as "the Emperor's schoolmaster." As the crestfallen electors skulked out of the Vatican, one observer wrote, "I thought I saw ghosts from limbo, so white and distraught were the faces I looked on. Almost all are dissatisfied, and repent already of having chosen a stranger, a barbarian, and a tutor of the Emperor."

The "stranger" was Adriaan Florensz, Adrian of Utrecht for short, and now Adrian VI. A sallow Dutchman sixty-two years of age, frugal, scholarly, and pious, completely unknown in Rome and utterly the antithesis of Leo X, he had been tutor to the youthful Charles V. At the time of his election he was cardinal in Tortosa, Spain. Significantly, he was also inquisitor-general of the dreaded Spanish Inquisition, successor to the dreadful duo of Tomás de Torquemada and Ximénes de Cisneros. It was to him and the ministrations of his star chamber that Leo X had proposed to send Luther, if only he could fall into the embrace of the church. Indeed, during the Diet of Worms Adrian had recommended to the emperor that Luther be seized there and sent immediately to Rome for punishment.

If mortification in Rome was great, nowhere was the sentiment greater than in Adrian himself in Vitoria, Spain. When he heard the news of his election on January 24, 1522, he pled his personal weakness, his age and uncertain health, and his inadequacy. His temperament was that of a scholar, he protested, not a leader.

Not everyone was upset at the news of Adrian's election. In the camp of Charles V there was quiet satisfaction. Beset by the three epic problems of the war in Italy, the Islamic invasion of Eastern Europe, and Luther's revolt, Charles remarked that he was sure he "could rely on the new Pope as thoroughly as on anyone who had risen to greatness of his service."

Far away in his monk's cell at the Wartburg, Luther was almost blasé. So toughened was he now to assaults and threats from
Rome that he could brush off the news of this vaunted election—
even the fact that the grand inquisitor of the Spanish Inquisition had been chosen pope. It was politics closer to home that
was on the Reformer's mind. From his letters it does not appear
that he even realized that with Leo's death he might now be released from a dire fate. Instead, his focus was on a project that
ultimately would have a far greater impact on world affairs than
the shenanigans in the Eternal City.

Thirteen

ALL ALONE

I N THE NEW YEAR, AS ROME WAS MIRED IN THE DYSFUNCTION of its papal election, Luther soldiered on with his monumental translation at the Wartburg. But he still felt overwhelmed. On January 14, 1522, he wrote to his friend Nicholas von Amsdorf. "I have given myself a burden that goes beyond my powers. Now I realize what it means to translate, and why no one, who would put his name to the work, has previously undertaken it."

But he would stick at it until Easter, he promised, and he was already projecting his mind forward to the translation of the Old Testament: "Of course, I will not be able to touch the Old Testament all by myself and without the cooperation of all of you. If it could somehow be arranged that I could have a secret room with any one of you, I would soon come and with your help would translate the whole book from the beginning, so that it would be a worthy translation for Christians to read. For I hope we will have a better translation for our Germany than the Latins have."

In his fatigue the Reformer might have returned to his translation of Matthew 11:28. The Vulgate read: "Come to me all you that labor and are burdened, and I will refresh you." Luther needed refreshment, but his rendering was different: "Come to me all you who are weary and burdened, and I will give you rest." Rest or refreshment: he needed them both.

After only five weeks of labor, he had finished the Gospels and the Acts, and was already focused on Paul's First Epistle to the Corinthians. And there, in 1 Corinthians 7:14, he confronted the issue of illegitimacy. Working from his mentor Erasmus's Greek translation, he came upon this passage: "For the unbelieving husband is sanctified by the believing wife; and the unbelieving wife is sanctified by the believing husband. Otherwise your children should be unclean: but now they are holy." Very possibly the passage brought Erasmus to mind, for the great humanist was himself an illegitimate child, and his birth had only been cleansed through a special papal dispensation in 1517. Were the children of a union involving one believer and one unbeliever illicit? On the same day he wrote to Amsdorf, Luther wrote to Melanchthon for his counsel.

"How do you understand that passage in 1 Corinthians 7:14?" he wondered. "Do we understand this as relevant only to adults, or to the sanctity of the flesh in general?" Regardless of parental belief or unbelief, did not baptism sanctify children? And did not this passage underscore the importance of a mixed marriage staying together for the sake of the children? Did the passage apply only to children or to adults as well? After some thought, Luther broadened the passage to read: "The unbelieving man is sanctified through his woman, and the unbelieving woman is sanctified through her man. Otherwise their children would be unclean. Now they are holy." This was a more expansive, liberal interpretation of the Scripture than any translation that had come before it, and it foreshadowed Luther's imminent work on another passage, one that would come to define his entire theology.

Luther's Cell at the Wartburg. Credit: Ulrich Kneise, Wartburg Foundation

THE THIRD CHAPTER OF PAUL'S LETTER TO THE ROMANS IS A reaffirmation of humanity's essential sinfulness, but it also addresses the question of how the sinful person might become righteous. Are humans simply to be eternally damned for their deceit and lies, and thus denied salvation? Or can a sinner redeem himself or herself somehow by faith and by good works? Of these two, faith or good works, which offered the true path to forgiveness and redemption? "Justification" was the central question. It referred to the process by which baleful sinners could transform themselves into just and righteous persons.

Luther saw his doctrine of justification as the nub of his theology, "the one and firm rock" of the entire Christian faith. Only through it could one understand God. Upon it the Christian Church stood or fell.

And so he came to Romans 3:23–24. In the received text of St. Jerome, the passage reads: "For all who have sinned and need the glory of God, being justified freely by his grace through the redemption of Jesus Christ." The King James Version would change the wording slightly: "For all have sinned, and come short of the glory of God; Being justified freely by his grace through the redemption that is in Christ Jesus."

What did this mean, to be justified freely through Christ's grace? How was the sinner to understand so obscure and abstract a concept?

Luther rewrote the passage: "Therefore we conclude that man is justified by faith alone."

His first rationalization for the change rested on the nature of the German language itself. The word "alone" was routinely used in such sentences as "I have alone eaten and not yet drunk." In his native tongue the word "alone" is added to make a sentence more complete and clear, he argued. "We do not have to ask literal Latin how to speak German, as these donkeys do," he wrote.

This radical interpretation established the preeminent concept of *sola fide*, faith alone. The notion had been evolving in his mind for years. It may, in fact, have had its roots in his training as an Augustinian monk and his identification with St. Augustine himself. Bishop Augustine of Hippo in the fourth century had been open about the licentiousness of his youth, about his battle with self-contempt and a sense of his own weakness, about his struggle against the temptations of his sexual nature. How had he achieved salvation? By his good works later?

In Luther's many good works up until this time in his life, he felt only emptiness and dissatisfaction. To be an upstanding, charitable person was not enough. Something deeper, more spiritual, more mystical was required for him or any other person to be saved. In the formulation of his concept of justification he had also been influenced by the work of a French humanist of the time, Jacques Lefèvre d'Étaples. In 1512 Lefèvre had written: "Let us not speak of the merit of our works which is little or nothing, but let us celebrate the grace of God which is everything."

Luther was elevating his concept of justification now to the central tenet of his Reformation. He meant for it to stand as the primary distinction between his new theology of salvation and the Roman Catholic emphasis on good works. It was for him a transformative moment, one he was sure was inspired by the Holy Spirit. When he solidified this concept in his mind, he proclaimed, "I felt altogether born again and had entered paradise itself through open gates."

In translating this one sentence and consciously adding the word "alone," Luther appreciated its revolutionary power. After he had finished translating the whole Letter to the Romans, he returned to this fundamental issue in his introduction to the Epistle. For a sinner to think that he could be saved by good works—a kind of mechanical accounting of good works over bad, credit for the good, debit for the bad—was a dream and a delusion, he wrote. The impulse to value good works was a human—not a divine—idea, a conscious, intellectual fantasy that by doing a host of good deeds, the sinner could escape damnation. Since the idea derives from the mind and not the heart, from the person and not from God, true "reform," personal or collective, does not flow from it.

To the Reformer, faith itself animates change. It denotes a personal, vibrant, immediate relation between the believer and the Almighty. "It is a living, creative, active, and powerful thing," Luther wrote. Almost incidentally, he might say, the truly reformed, faithful person cannot help doing good works. His doctrine was far from passive. It was not a question of one or another, faith or good works. But deep faith drove a person to do good works automatically. It was the essence and the catalyst. And so he wrote,

"It is just as impossible to separate faith and works as it is to separate heat and light from fire!"

Fourteen

FANATICS TAKE OVER

I
F LUTHER HAD LEFT WITTENBERG IN MID-DECEMBER 1521
with a certain comfort about the state of affairs there, no
sooner was he out of town than the situation again veered out
of control. Andreas Karlstadt reasserted his aggressive bid for the
helm of the Reformation, pushing the movement into deeper and
more dangerous waters than Luther was prepared to take it, and
risking the opposition of ordinary believers by enforcing radical
measures in the liturgy and the practice of their Protestant faith.
The foundation for fundamental change had not yet been laid,
Luther felt.

Once Luther left Wittenberg, Karlstadt announced his intention to hold an evangelical Lord's Supper on New Year's Day that
would flout traditional practices and feature the novelties. When
Elector Frederick stepped in to forbid the spectacle, Karlstadt
moved the celebration forward to Christmas Day. With this license students stormed the churches, broke lamps, and chanted
for plague and fire to rain down on the heads of all priests. At
the Christmas Day service at the Castle Church, Karlstadt said
the Mass without vestments, omitted the adoration of Christ in

171

the canon, and allowed the congregants to take the chalice into their own hands to drink the blood of Christ. He proclaimed that marriage was obligatory for priests, and a day later, he announced he would marry the fifteen-year-old daughter of an indigent nobleman.

Meanwhile, in towns surrounding Wittenberg, the radical monk Gabriel Zwilling was conducting evangelical Masses, dressed in student attire with a jaunty feather in his cap. Confessions were stopped. The law of fasting was disregarded. Religious comfort for the sick ended. And it was proposed to terminate all feast days except Sundays.

At the same time, in the south of Saxony, a new challenge to the movement emerged. In Zwickau, a substantial, mercantile town of seven thousand noted for its cloth making, a different revolt was brewing. Sympathy for Luther was strong there, especially among itinerant cloth workers, who bridled at the gulf between the rich and the poor of the town. They gravitated to a firebrand preacher named Thomas Müntzer, who initially had been promoted by Luther within the ranks of the priesthood.

Müntzer was a demagogue of the first order. Silver-tongued and excitable, with piercing eyes and hair cascading in curls over his shoulders, he openly proclaimed his desire to rouse the ghost of the heretic Jan Huss. His contempt for established priests was absolute. He preached against indulgences, purgatory, celibacy, and Masses for the dead, and poured his fire down on his working-class followers with unparalleled passion. "Man has long hungered for divine justice," he ranted. "The children have called for bread, and there has been no one to cut it for them. Look at those who toss texts from the Bible to them like dogs. We shall see if your Mass-mumblers are real priests. Wretched pastors, whose paps are so dried up that they have no more milk to offer their lambs . . . storks that gobble up the poor frogs who by ill luck dwell in swamps . . . birds of prey who feed their young with stones in the shape of food. . . .

"I tell you that the lands of the North are about to be watered with the river of grace. The Church shall be renewed and extend its kingdom over the whole world. Do not come to me . . . come to God. In the name of the crimson blood of Christ I urge you to compare me with your priests in Rome. I, Müntzer, demand that the Church shall cease to pray to dumb gods."

Müntzer had formed an alliance with a master cloth cutter named Nicolas Storch. Dour, colorless, but clear in his vision, Storch was a man learned in the Bible who claimed to have a special, direct relationship to the Almighty and who spoke of having divine revelations and magical illuminations. Around Zwickau, he was holding secret gatherings of his chosen followers outside of the church, occasioning a few riots. He strode about in a wide-brimmed hat and a long, gray robe, flattering the simple folk for their instinctive wisdom and urging them to carry "the blood-red banner against all authority."

"Behold what I announce to you," he exclaimed. "During the night, God sent his angel to me who said I shall sit upon the same throne as Gabriel. Let the wicked tremble! Let the righteous hope! The wicked shall be crushed, and God's elect shall be king on earth. Heaven has promised the empire of the world to me. Do you wish to be visited by God like me? Prepare your hearts to receive the Holy Ghost. Let there be no more pulpits to announce the World of God, no more priests or books. Let your clothing be simple, your food coarse, and God will descend upon you."

The Holy Spirit was calling him to purify the church of the "godless" completely before the End Times.

Between the aggressive preaching of Müntzer, the apocalyptic rants of Storch, and the civil unrest, the town council of Zwickau became alarmed. Complaints were lodged with both Duke George the Bearded in Leipzig and Duke John the Steady in Torgau. Investigations were launched. But before anything could be done, Müntzer fled to Prague. In turn, Storch and two other ringleaders escaped to Wittenberg, where they set about poisoning the very heart of Luther's movement.

Calling themselves "men of inner light," Storch and his companions arrived in Wittenberg on December 27 and immediately became the talk of the town.

On the day of their arrival, the gullible Melanchthon wrote to Elector Frederick, "I have examined them and must confess they speak wonderful things. In truth, I have good cause not to reject them." The ferocious certitude of the Zwickauers captivated Luther's timid surrogate; their representations of divine revelation intimidated and fascinated him.

"Who commissioned you to preach?" Melanchthon had asked.

"The Lord," Storch had replied. This was a problem, for within the nascent theology of the Reformation, this was technically an acceptable answer. Had not Luther, in *The Babylonian Captivity of the Church*, proclaimed every man to be a preacher with his concept of the universal priesthood? So why not this man?

The fanatics found immediate, enthusiastic favor with Karlstadt as well. Dramatically, the leading intellectual of Wittenberg had transformed himself into a primitivist, valuing direct inspiration over textbooks and commentaries and even the Bible itself. But the task of dealing with this direct challenge to the cause fell to Philipp Melanchthon. While the "little Greek" was initially gullible, his spine was stiffening.

Of special difficulty for the Reformation, theologically speaking, was the Zwickau radicals' rejection of infant baptism. It was a question that the Luther's followers had yet to address: whether innocent toddlers really understood the meaning of the sacrament when they were baptized, and if not, could they really be considered true believers. In Luther's mind baptism was one of the two authentic sacraments, along with the Eucharist. In Catholicism this ritual was universally used to usher children into the faith. But did they really comprehend what was happening?

The "prophets" were touching on a weak point of Luther's evolving theology, to wit, that infant baptism was inconsistent with the core principle of justification by faith alone. Luther himself would say later, "I have always expected the Devil would touch this sore point. But he would not do it through the papists. We ourselves are in great conflict concerning it."

THE UNSETTLING PRESENCE OF THE SPIRITUALISTS ALSO alarmed Elector Frederick, who was having enough trouble keeping the peace in his house without this further disruption. "Everything has gone wrong," he bemoaned. "Everybody is perplexed, and no one knows who is the cook and who is the cellarist."

On New Year's Day, 1522, Frederick gathered his advisers—Melanchthon, Amsdorf, and Spalatin—to decide what to do. Melanchthon suggested that the challenge was perplexing enough to warrant recalling Luther from the Wartburg, since only he had the competence and the stature to confront this new aggravation. But Frederick did not think it was safe yet to bring Luther back to Wittenberg. At the same time the elector, still nominally a Catholic, wanted to steer clear of theological disputes, not only the question of infant baptism but also the questions of celibacy and the abolition of the Mass.

Melanchthon sat on the fence. "I expected that the Devil would attack us on this weak point," he remarked. While he had finally come to doubt the claims of divine inspiration, he was deeply troubled about the assault on infant baptism. Amsdorf, for his part, thought the Zwickau prophets might, indeed, represent an authentic outpouring of the Holy Ghost before the apocalypse and the last days.

As a stopgap measure the elector ordered his advisers to ignore the prophets and have nothing further to do with them.

On Epiphany, the annual celebration on January 6 of Christ's revelation as the son of God, a thousand congregants gathered to celebrate the Mass in the new way and to hear Karlstadt rattle the rafters. The arch deacon proclaimed that confession before communion was unnecessary and that previous rules about fasting were null and void. He denounced begging and railed against the icons and images of saints in the church to be sacrilegious idolatry. He declared baptism of infants to be invalid, so that adult baptism might be required. He announced his marriage date for two weeks from that day, January 19. Most shockingly, he adopted the position of the prophets that direct illumination by the Holy Spirit was possible, making scholarship unnecessary for understanding Scripture. In this final declaration he subscribed to the Zwickau emphasis on a certain passage in Exodus: "You shall have no other gods but me. You shall not make unto yourself any graven image or any likeness of any thing that is in heaven above or that is in the earth beneath, or that is in the water under the earth. You shall not bow down to them, nor serve them: for the Lord God is a jealous God" (20:3–5).

Shortly thereafter, with Wittenberg magistrates looking the other way and Gabriel Zwilling leading the charge, a mob descended on the churches of the town and systematically destroyed all the altars and icons. Ironically, the image of mammon, the deity of wealth and greed, was left untouched. To justify this curious omission the mantra of the mob was a passage from Luke 16:13: "No man can serve two masters, for either he will hate the one and love the other; or else he will hold to the one, and despise the other. You cannot serve God and mammon."

Karlstadt destroys church icons. By Willem Linnig. CREDIT: ULRICH KNEISE, WARTBURG FOUNDATION

The reputation of Wittenberg as a refuge for all fanatics was spreading far and wide. The Reformation risked being branded as nothing more than a cult of looters and lunatics. The struggle for the future of the movement was entering a desperate phase.

Inevitably, Melanchthon and his brothers turned to the master. On January 13, 1522, Luther sent his response. In a letter to Amsdorf he seemed almost cavalier. His followers should not worry too much about the zealots—he would patronize them later as *Schwarmgeister* or the "dreamers"—and he was not of a mind to return to Wittenberg over them. They might boast about their special gift for communicating with God, but he very much doubted that they were having any direct or indirect conversations with the Almighty. On the same day, in a letter to Melanchthon, Luther addressed the issue more pointedly. Sensing that his surrogate had been dazzled by the "prophets"—Luther always put the word in quotes—he again berated his friend for his insecurity and indecisiveness, while at the same time seeking to shore him up. "You are stronger in spirit and learning than I," he wrote. Melanchthon was fully capable of dealing with the emergency.

The critical thing, Luther told Melanchthon, was to test the claims of the provocateurs. If they spoke only of pleasant and quiet conversations with God, saying nothing about spiritual distress or suffering the pangs of hell that leads to rebirth, then he doubted their validity. In other words, "examine them. Do not even listen if they speak only of the glorified Christ, unless you have first heard them speak of the crucified Christ." God never speaks directly to people, Luther asserted, but only indirectly through human intermediaries. He cited the example of the prophet Samuel in 1 Samuel 3:4–14. "God speaks through men indirectly," Luther wrote, "because not all can endure his speaking. The angel frightened even the Virgin, and also Daniel."

On the question of infant baptism, Luther was equally blunt. He held to the line in Mark 16:16, "He that believeth and is baptized shall be saved." How could these "prophets" prove that children do not believe? he asked. "Children also participate in the benefits and promise of Christ." Baptism was free and available to all people of every age. Faith was infused into the child at baptism, and this infusion was a singular miracle of God. No priest, nor even heretic, had ever raised his voice against the practice until now.

"Is it not that in baptism the child becomes the participator in the merits of Christ?" he asked.

Three days later, in a letter to Spalatin, as the elector's lieutenant, Luther dealt with the practical aspects of the Zwickau provocation. Even if it were true that the "prophets" had incited students to riot and inspired Karlstadt to go off the deep end, he did not want them attacked or jailed. "Please see to it that our Sovereign does not stain his hands with the blood of these new 'prophets' from Zwickau," he wrote, for "they do not disturb me."

The Zwickau prophets may not have disturbed Luther, not at that time anyway, but in Wittenberg their presence had contributed to what historians now call the Wittenberg Disturbances, the collective uprisings that took place around the turn of 1521 and early 1522. The Reformer had underestimated the mischief these interlopers had done. In his absence things were spiraling out of control.

No doubt Luther reflected on the past eight months and the role he played in these disturbing events. He had hammered relentlessly at the Catholic edifice. He had argued that celibacy was the inspiration of the Devil; he promoted marriage for priests; he claimed that purgatory was a deceit, that monastic vows were a human invention, that the Mass was no sacrifice; he had set out to remake the Catholic Bible. As he took these iconoclastic positions, he had been debilitated by physical illness, attacked by Catholics at all levels, and rebuked by kings, university professors, and the pope. He had seen his books burned, and he had been threatened with immolation on the stake.

Or as he put it: "With fire, wood, and coal, burn the rash fool!"

Now the tables had been turned on him by his own disciples and his naïve followers, and Luther saw the hand of the Devil at work. "Satan has slipped into my flock in Wittenberg," he wrote a few weeks later. He had lost faith in Melanchthon's ability to lead in his absence. As it happened, unbeknown to Luther, the three Zwickau prophets had all left Wittenberg by January 6, but their influence remained acrid in the air of Wittenberg, and Luther would feel compelled to deal with their nefarious influence later. Fanatics were different from Christians, he would say, for Christians are always open to doubt, whereas fanatics hold firm to their beliefs and never change. Therein lay their power.

At the Wartburg he slept no more than two or three hours a night and spent his waking hours in correspondence and translating, but it was not enough. At home his message was unraveling. Daily he heard about ever "wilder things." He began to think of returning to Wittenberg before he finished translating the New Testament. His movement was in real jeopardy.

"Lord willing, I shall definitely return in a short time," he informed Spalatin.

Fifteen

LIBERATION

ON JANUARY 22, 1522, A NEW, DANGEROUS DEVELOPMENT altered Luther's situation dramatically. Prodded by Duke George of Saxony, Luther's most treacherous foe, the Imperial Council of Regency in Nürnberg, issued a mandate demanding that all innovations in Saxon churches cease immediately or be forcibly suppressed under the threat of severe punishment. Specifically, priests were ordered to preach publicly against the novelties. Karlstadt and the radical Augustinian Gabriel Zwilling were held directly responsible for the Wittenberg Disturbances, although implicitly Luther was held ultimately accountable. That the radical pair were not authorized to preach at all was underscored: they were forbidden to do so again. Amsdorf was officially appointed as preacher at the city church under strict guidelines. Imperial officers were dispatched to investigate any church that had been reported as having strayed from the Catholic liturgy.

The suppression of Luther's novelties and their radical offshoots had taken a serious turn. The authorities, both Vatican and imperial, were finally mobilizing against the Reformation and its adherents.

Within days, Luther heard of the new draconian measures, and he immediately appreciated their significance. "No one can deny that the present commotion has its origin in me," he wrote. Already, as tales of violence and vandalism reached him from Wittenberg, the imperative to abandon his Patmos grew ever stronger in his mind. He could no longer manage or control things at a distance with his pen alone. His confused, buffeted flock needed to hear from him in the flesh. With the imperial police possibly on the way to Wittenberg, he must have worried that he had waited too long.

For his entire stay "in the wilderness," Luther had communicated with Elector Frederick through his court chaplain, George Spalatin. Now direct communication was required, lest there be any mistake in translation. On February 22, therefore, Luther settled on the slender pretext of congratulating the elector on acquiring yet another holy relic for his voluminous collection. It was a cross studded with nails and festooned with spears and scourges. In his letter to the elector Luther implied that the relic was a metaphor for the troubles in Wittenberg and that Frederick should take care not to be crucified by them himself. His sovereign should be wise and prudent and not be discouraged by the unrest. "Do not be downhearted, for things have not yet come to pass as Satan wishes," the monk wrote.

In the last few sentences of the brief letter, Luther came to the point: his return was imminent. "I am in such haste that my pen has had to gallop," he wrote. "I have not time for more. God willing I shall soon be there. But Your Grace must not assume responsibility for me." The last sentence required elaboration, but for the moment Luther offered none.

His pen was indeed galloping, for he was coming to the end of his translation and needed a little more time. He had come to the last chapters of the New Testament, which he had always considered the lesser books: the Epistle of James, the Epistle of St. Jude, the Epistle of Paul to the Hebrews, and most significantly, the Book of Revelation. Were they really Holy Scripture at all? he asked himself. A major restructuring of the New Testament seemed to be in order. An appendix was his solution.

"We should throw the Epistle of James out of this school, for it doesn't amount to much," he exclaimed. "It contains not a syllable about Christ."

Moreover, he doubted that the apostle James had actually written the Epistle that bore his name. The Epistle mangled the Scriptures, Luther felt. It made no mention of the Passion, the resurrection, or the spirit of Christ. In the Gospel of John, Chapter 15, Christ had said to his apostles, "You shall bear witness to me." All the genuine sacred books after the Gospels demonstrated this witness, and that was the true test of authenticity. Whatever book did not teach about Christ is not apostolic, Luther decided. The author of the Epistle of James was probably a pious man who came long after St. Paul, but he harped too much on the law rather than the spirit. And his work was thrown together "chaotically" by taking a few sayings from the followers of the disciples and then tossing them off on paper.

"Therefore, I will not have him in my Bible as a true chief book," he decided. It was a good book with some good sayings, he conceded, but it was not holy. Both Erasmus and even St. Jerome himself had also doubted the authenticity of the Epistle, and so Luther felt himself to be on solid ground in downgrading its significance.

Dealing with the Epistle of St. Jude was easy, for it was unquestionably an extract of St. Peter's Second Epistle with many identical words. After the death of Christ Jude the apostle went east to Persia and then Syria, where he was martyred. So how could he write a Greek letter? In excluding Jude's Epistle,

Luther was merely following the example of the ancient fathers, who had done likewise. Therefore, in his taut German Bible, Luther could easily move it to the back as redundant and unnecessary.

His doubts about the Epistle of Paul to the Hebrews were different. While he would praise the book faintly as a "marvelously fine epistle" that "interprets the Old Testament in a fine way" and deals with Scriptures "in the proper way," its authorship was certainly not Paul or another apostle, but some anonymous person who came afterwards. The second chapter of Hebrews (2:3) proved it; there the author wrote about words spoken by the Lord and "confirmed to us by those who heard him." The writer would probably never be known, Luther decided, but never mind. It made no difference. To the back of the book it went.

Luther saved his most fundamental objection for the last book of the New Testament, the Book of Revelation. In it he found no evidence of the presence of the Holy Spirit whatsoever, much less that of the apostles. Whereas the apostles taught about the foundation of faith and about the life of Jesus, this book said nothing about Christ but rather dealt in obscure, phantasmagoric images and visions that were neither apostolic nor prophetic. It threatened destruction for any who did not take to heart its lessons and warnings, and yet, said Luther, no one including himself could understand how to keep its hallucinatory teaching.

Here Luther could even take issue with his mentor and the original translator of the Bible into Latin. St. Jerome had spoken of the profound mysteries of the Book of Revelation. The saint could not prove its profundity, Luther responded, and his praise was over-generous.

With these major decisions about structure decided, Luther could turn back to practical matters.

Several days after his February 22 letter to Elector Frederick signaling his imminent return to Wittenberg, Luther received a plea he could no longer ignore. His Wittenberg church and its council, including Cranach, Melanchthon, and Amsdorf, urgently and formally requested the Reformer to return. Melanchthon was the driving force behind the request, but Amsdorf was the most desperate.

"Come or we perish," he wrote.

"Yes, I will come," Luther answered. "God calls me. I hear his voice. My children in Jesus Christ are there. I will be guilty of their blood if I do not go to their rescue. For them I am ready to suffer everything, even death. Satan has taken advantage of my absence to create disturbances among my sheep. I will snatch them from him, for they are mine. My pen is useless here."

Reading Luther's February 22 letter, Frederick could now have no doubt that Luther was preparing to leave, and the elector had grave misgivings about the wisdom of the move. In the unsettled situation he could not be sure that he could protect the Reformer—not only from the emperor's agents but even from the radicals in Wittenberg. If a formal request came from the emperor to seize the fugitive, Frederick would be hard-pressed to refuse for political reasons. Doing so would undermine his authority.

And so Frederick ordered the bailiff of Eisenach to climb the hill to the Wartburg and do his best to dissuade Luther from leaving the castle, or at least to persuade him to postpone his departure indefinitely. To a scowling Luther the bailiff made the arguments: the situation in Wittenberg was confusing, unsettled, and dangerous; it would not be wise for Luther to be seen in public just now; the elector's powers to protect him were limited; Luther's presence in Wittenberg could lead to further violence; and so on.

The meeting did not go well. Luther departed the next day.

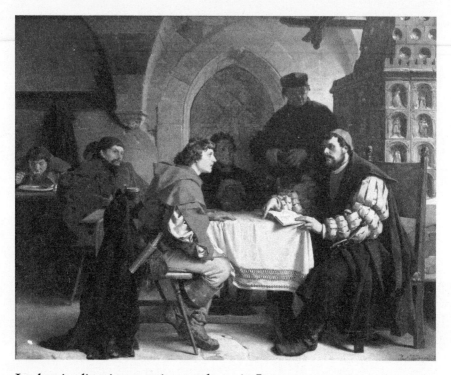

Luther in disguise meeting students in Jena. CREDIT: ULRICH KNEISE,
WARTBURG FOUNDATION

The monk's 175-mile journey from Eisenach to Wittenberg
took eight days. He charted a roundabout southerly route, traveling alone to the eastern edge of Thuringen, avoiding the perilous
Saxon dominion of Duke George for as long as he could. Instead
of opting for plain clothes that might render him invisible, he
made himself conspicuous in the guise of a traveling cavalier,
with buckled sword, a close-fitting doublet, slim knickers to the
knee, and a jaunty red beret. At the bar at the Black Bear Inn in
Jena (the Hotel Schwarzer Bär still exists there) he settled in for
a drink, thumbing through a Hebrew Psalter in his lap.

Soon enough he fell into conversation with several Swiss di-
vinity students, who, as it happened, were on their way to Wit-

tenberg for further religious studies and—they hoped—to meet the great Martin Luther. They hailed from St. Gallen, a famous center for artists and iconoclasts. Junker Jörg plied them with copious advice, including his encouragement that they study Greek and Hebrew if they really wanted to understand the Bible. When, in the course of the *klatsch*, he sprinkled his speech with a few Latin phrases, the students knew they were in the company of a very unusual knight. There was something about his eyes. "His eyes were black and deep," one of the students wrote later. "They sparkled and flashed like a star, so that they could not easily be met."

"What do people in Switzerland think of Luther?" the knight asked the students. Opinion was split, they replied. Some regarded him highly, while others saw him as a dangerous heretic. The encounter ended on a happy note, with the generous knight paying the students' bill. And by the way, the students said, they hoped to meet the great man of Wittenberg who had so changed the Mass. Did the knight happen to know if Martin Luther was then in Wittenberg?

"I know quite positively that he is not there now," the knight replied, "but he soon will be there."

Passing into the dangerous Catholic zone of Duke George, where with every step he might be seized, he accepted two knights as escorts and proceeded to the town of Borna south of Duke George's domicile in Leipzig. The protection of these escorts was a far cry from the support he had been offered previously. Franz von Sickingen, his powerful military supporter after the Diet of Worms, was unavailable, preoccupied far away in the Rhineland with mobilizing an army in what would be called the Knights' Revolt against the archbishops of the Roman church. (He would be killed in battle a year later.) Luther's other military champion, Sylvester von Schaumberg, was somewhere to the

south in Franconia and engaged in a similar campaign to mobilize provincial knights. Despite the danger, Luther was disdainful
toward his potential executioner, Duke George, and professed to
have prayed for and wept for the "Hog of Dresden" more than
once, in the hope that his prayer might enlighten his nemesis
and dissipate the duke's wrath. But he would not waste too much
breath on the effort. At the same time he did not savor the possibility of falling into Duke George's clutches.

At Borna he sat down to write to Elector Frederick again. It
was as if he felt compelled, as he rode to his possible martyrdom,
to explain his disobedience and also to relieve his protector of
any guilt or responsibility, should he be captured in the next few
days. His March 5 letter to Frederick is among the most famous
he ever wrote. He began with the usual obsequies. For the elector, he wrote, he had more affection and respect than any other
sovereign or ruler on earth. But the calamity in Wittenberg had
overwhelmed and pained him, since the arbitrary innovations
were a great detriment to the gospel. "If I had not been certain
that we have the pure gospel"—a gospel he had received directly
from Jesus Christ, he asserted—"I would have despaired of our
cause." His "excessive humility" had kept him in exile at the
Wartburg, and he had served the elector well by staying in hiding
for nearly a year to please him.

"All the harm previously done me in this cause has been a
joke, a mere nothing. Had it been possible I would willingly have
given my life to prevent it. For we can justify what has been done
neither before God nor before the world."

But now he saw that he had made a mistake in staying away so
long. He had to act. The elector must know that he was coming
to Wittenberg under a far higher authority than Frederick's. "I
have no intention of asking Your Electoral Grace for protection,"
he stated flatly. "Indeed, I shall protect Your Electoral Grace

more than you can protect me. If I thought that you could and would protect me, I should not come. The sword cannot help a matter like this. God alone must do it, without the cooperation of men. He who believes the most can protect the most. Since I have the impression that Your Electoral Grace is still weak in faith, I cannot regard you as the man to protect and save me."

Since he had disobeyed the elector (and was now rebuking him for his weak Catholic faith), he accepted full responsibility for his actions and relieved Frederick of any moral blame, should he be seized and put to death. If Emperor Charles V moved to arrest him, the elector was to offer no resistance. "No one should overthrow or resist authority, save him who ordained it," Luther wrote. "Otherwise it is rebellion and an action against God." And if the papists or the imperialists laid hands on him, he would see to it that the elector suffered no repercussions on his account.

Having thus justified his actions to his patron, Luther sent off the letter and continued on his way toward Wittenberg, ready to meet whatever fate awaited him there.

When he arrived outside Wittenberg, the Reformer changed into his black monk's habit and proceeded to the Augustinian monastery, which was now nearly empty.

In the decades to come, Luther's return to Wittenberg from the Wartburg would become the stuff of legend. Artists portrayed his perilous journey in heroic terms. A woodcut showed him en route preceded by a winged serpent, the symbol of salvation, and the heraldic design of Elector Frederick's seal, taken from John 3:14–15: "As Moses lifted up the serpent in the wilderness, even so much the son of man be lifted up, that whosoever believes in him shall not perish, but have everlasting life." Lucas Cranach portrayed Luther entering Wittenberg dressed in his warrior's costume; at the bottom of the painting's frame were Luther's own words:

So often have I been harassed
So often have I been attacked by you, Rome
Behold, I, Luther, through Christ, still live!

Yet it was not Rome now that threatened Luther, but the temporal authority of the emperor, Charles V. Would the emperor finally insist that the Edict of Worms be executed and, more than the mere lip service of the past, dispatch imperial soldiers to Wittenberg to back up his demand?

In his ducal castle in Wittenberg, Frederick learned of Luther's arrival shortly after the monk entered the town. Since the elector still professed to be a Roman Catholic and therefore could not publicly suffer a heretic to exist in his land, and since his domain was subordinate to imperial power, Frederick was in a tight spot. He was prepared to tolerate Luther in his midst, and to protect him quietly as he was able. But he wished formally to discourage the Reformer from further roiling the volatile situation in Wittenberg with inflammatory rhetoric.

When the elector was informed of Luther's arrival, he demanded that the monk write another letter promptly, one that could mollify the Imperial Council of the Regency in Nürnberg and discourage military action. The letter was to be addressed to Frederick but written for the eyes of the Imperial Council, and its purpose was to "maintain our honor." It was to set forth the reasons and motivations for Luther's precipitous return to Wittenberg without the elector's permission. "In order to maintain our honor," Frederick demanded, Luther was to state his willingness to exercise self-restraint and say he did not wish to instigate any trouble.

Luther complied immediately. He sympathized with the burden he had caused the elector by his return and acknowledged that he was banned and condemned by both papal and imperial law. Therefore, he expected death at any moment. But "God compels and calls me," he proclaimed. He harbored no contempt for Frederick or the emperor—he did not mention the pope. "Human authority is not always to be obeyed especially when it contradicts the commandments of God. Yet it should never be despised but always honored." Frederick, Luther wrote, was lord only of earthly goods and bodies, but Christ is lord of souls. "For these he has sent me."

In his new letter to Frederick Luther put forward three reasons for his return in contravention of the elector's wishes. First, his Wittenberg congregation had called him urgently, and as he was their humble servant, his parishioners' request could not be refused without rejecting Christian love. Given the commotion in the church, he was sure there were some who smiled at the chaos, hoping it would lead to the total demise of his movement. But "what I have begun does not originate in me, but in God." The work could not be allowed to perish.

Second, Luther wrote, Satan had slyly ingratiated himself into his congregation. He and only he had to deal personally with the Devil's agents. "My conscience will not allow me to yield or procrastinate further," he wrote. If he could deal with Satan's intrusion only by writing letters, he would have gladly done so, even to the extent of staying away from Wittenberg forever. But letters were no longer effective.

And third, he feared the possibility of rebellion in Germany. That would be God's punishment for a wicked land. There were those who were embittering people's hearts and provoking unrest. He and the elector needed to work together to erect "a wall of protection for the people." And so Luther was presenting himself as a peacemaker who could help to restore public order.

In closing Luther beseeched Frederick—and by implication the Imperial Council of the Regency—to exercise restraint and not hold his presence in Wittenberg against him. "The cause of the Gospel is in need," he proclaimed.

Elector Frederick received this letter as a draft and had Spalatin edit out its provocative passages. Luther had written about the council: "Something absolutely different was decided in heaven than at Nürnberg. Unfortunately, those gluttons who are gourmandizing the Gospel have not yet even begun to eat." Spalatin excised this gratuitous taunt and, at the elector's suggestion, removed the word "Nürnberg" and replaced it with the words "on earth." Within a few days the elector forwarded the softer version of Luther's letter to the Imperial Council in Nürnberg.

For the time being the crisis eased, and Luther could at last turn to his paramount calling to Wittenberg: to address his flock and to drive the devils from their midst.

Sixteen

CONSOLIDATION

THREE DAYS AFTER HIS ARRIVAL IN WITTENBERG, LUTHER was slated to give the first sermon of his homecoming. It was the first Sunday in Lent, Invocavit Sunday, as it is known in the Catholic calendar, taking its Latin word from the opening prayer for that day in the liturgy. As the great Reformer arrived at the town church and ascended its wooden pulpit, adorned with simple carvings of St. Matthew and St. John, the anticipation was enormous. A huge crowd had gathered, and without question Andreas Karlstadt lurked somewhere in the throng, perhaps peeking out from behind a pillar.

The importance of this first appearance since Luther had vanished on the road from Worms was enormous. Having experienced unrest in the autumn and riots in the winter, the Wittenberg church was in terrible disarray. Confusion reigned over Karlstadt's innovations. The town had had its wild carnival of radicalism; now came the solemnity of Lent and the return to sanity.

At all costs, Luther had to reassert control over his vulnerable movement, lest it burn itself out in a frenzy of overindulgence and negativism—and tempt military intervention. The imperial injunction had everyone in Wittenberg looking over their shoulders for the arrival of the imperial soldiers. The need to restore peace and unity and security was paramount. Just as important for Luther was to redefine the essentials of his Reformation, or in his words, "to know and be armed with the chief things that concern a Christian."

How would Luther conduct his Mass? Would he churn the waters further or seek to calm them? What would he have to say about his exile or the destruction of the idols or priestly marriages or celibacy or all of the radical experiments that had been sanctioned in his absence? It could escape no one that their great leader and mentor remained in extreme peril. As soon as he climbed the steps to the pulpit, would an imperial agent come right after him, clap him in irons, and drag him away? In short, the fate of his rebellion as well as the fate of Luther himself was at stake.

FROM THE BEGINNING THE SERVICE WAS ABNORMAL. DRESSED in the black robe of his Augustinian order, Luther blessed the congregation in the customary way but did not invoke the Holy Virgin. He dispensed with the usual preliminaries and moved quickly to his homily. Uncharacteristically, in his hand he held a sheaf of papers that bespoke his exacting preparation and the importance of his speaking precisely. Given the stakes, it had to be a bravura performance. From the first words that poured from his mouth, it was clear that he would be speaking not only to his flock but also about himself.

"The call to death comes to us all, and no one can die for another," Luther began. "Everyone must fight his own battle with death, alone. Everyone must himself be prepared for the time of death, for I will not be with you then, nor will you be with me."

What followed, on this day and in his sermons in the next seven days, was a delicate balance between uplifting inspiration and gentle reproach, delivered with wit and humor, firmness and wisdom. His method of preaching was to watch people's faces as he spoke, to see if the congregants were understanding his message.

His delivery gravitated to concrete, colorful, and emotional language. His first priority was to reestablish a sense of community and solidarity to his battered Wittenberg flock—and to reassert his leadership of it. By solidifying his congregation in their Reformation beliefs, he would be restoring the Wittenberg congregation as a paragon, presenting a unified identity to the world. They were journeying together in their mutual quest for truth and forgiveness and salvation, he asserted, sprinkling the first person plural—"we," "us," "our"—throughout his sermons. For they were all, including him, "children of wrath," evoking Paul's Epistle to the Ephesians 2:3: sinners in the "lusts of our flesh." As he was committed to them—"I love you even as I love my own soul," he said—so he hoped they would be committed to him and to his message. To strengthen the bond between them he addressed them often as "my friends," especially after he had said something harsh or critical.

At the outset he set the foundation for both religious belief and ethical behavior. They must remember the "chief things": faith, love, and patience. How each of them treated their neighbor was the key to the ethical structure he put forward. They should treat their neighbor as God had treated them and give to the poor, helping those at the margins of society to feel secure, especially when they are in crisis. "My friends," he told them, "each of you must see how he can help and benefit his brother. We must associate ourselves with our weaker brothers, be patient with them, not browbeat them cruelly but treat them in a kind and friendly way, instructing them gently."

The reproaches came randomly, salted into soaring passages as if he were merely laying the groundwork for more pointed criticism to come. "My friends, have you not grievously failed? I see no signs of love among you." Those who had erred in abolishing the private Mass did not err because it was a bad thing, he said, but because it was not done in an orderly fashion. It was done wantonly and rashly without regard for proper order and without being sensitive to one's neighbor. It was a "loveless exercise of liberty." Again, his identification of himself with Jesus was overt, especially Jesus on the verge of his martyrdom: "Dear brothers, I have never been a destroyer. I was the very first whom God called to his work. I cannot run away, but will remain as long as God allows. I was also the one to whom God first revealed that his Word should be preached to you. I am sure that you have the pure Word of God."

They must be careful, he said, that Wittenberg did not become Capernaum, that village exalted as the site where Jesus delivered the Sermon on the Mount and healed the sick, the village that was the center of His ministry in Galilee, just as Wittenberg was the center of Luther's ministry in Saxony. Capernaum had proved itself to be unrepentant, and therefore Jesus had cursed it: "And thou, Capernaum, which art exalted unto heaven, shalt be brought down to hell" (Matthew 11:23). Wittenberg must not be allowed to be dragged down to hell, as Capernaum had been.

Why had they not consulted with him about the novelties? He was not far away and could have received a letter, but no letter had come. "Therefore, I could no longer remain away, but was compelled to come and say these things to you," he chastised.

In his second sermon his speech was more conversational and intimate, even as his criticism of the novelties became sharper. His doting followers looked at him in hushed awe. Beyond the forcefulness of his speech was the simple clarity with which he made the issues understandable. They remarked on his voice. It was sweet, sonorous, hypnotic. And on his temperament: it was kind, gentle, and cheerful. A convert to the Zwickau prophets quietly dropped his support as he listened to this "angel." One of the Swiss students he had met in Jena was struck again by Luther's extraordinary eyes. "His deep-set black eyes blinked and twinkled like stars, so that it was uncomfortable to behold them," he wrote. Another observer saw Luther's intense gaze differently: "His eyes have a certain sinister sparkle, such as one finds from time to time in persons who are possessed by the Devil."

The opening passage of his second sermon focused on compulsion. "I cannot push anybody into heaven, not even with stick beating," he said. His followers need to distinguish between things of necessity and things of choice, or in his words the difference between "must" and "free." Their evangelism should never be forced on anyone. To compel belief in their doctrine would make their message into a mockery, rendering them hypocrites. They must first win the hearts of the people through persuasion, not force. "I cannot, nor should I, force anyone to have faith." That was God's work, and the results had to be left to His pleasure. "Look what I have done!" he cried. "Have I not done more damage to the pope, bishops, priests and monks with my tongue alone, without one stroke of the sword, than all the emperors and kings with all their might?"

And then came the crowd pleaser: "I have done more harm to the pope while sleeping, or drinking beer in a Wittenberg alehouse with Philipp and Amsdorf than all the princes and emperors together." One can almost hear the laughter and the cheers echoing from the walls of the church. But what he said next would quiet them. "If I loved commotion, how much blood I could have caused to be shed in Europe!" he exclaimed. "Would the emperor himself have been safe at Worms if I had not spared his life? But what would have been the result? It would have been madness, corrupting both body and soul. I did nothing and let the Word do its work."

For the next five days he continued to preach to them from his reclaimed pulpit. In the seventh sermon he returned to the theme of love. Between faith and love, he told them, there is a necessary relationship. One without the other was emptiness. To have faith without love was a counterfeit of faith; indeed, it was not faith at all. It was like a face seen in a mirror: not a real face, but merely a reflection of a face. In this image he was prompted by Paul's verse, 1 Corinthians 13:12–13: "We see through a glass, darkly . . . and now abideth faith, hope, charity . . . but the greatest of these is charity." He constantly used Scripture to legitimize his arguments.

Love, he said, is the fruit of the sacrament. "From God we have received nothing but love and favor. He has poured out upon us all his treasures which no man can measure and no angel can fathom, for God is a glowing furnace of love." They must share their love rather than keep it to themselves. And then he delivered a stiff admonition: "If you will not love one another, God will send a great plague upon you. Let this be a warning to you, for God will not have his Word revealed and preached in vain."

TAKEN TOGETHER, HIS EIGHT BACK-TO-BACK HOMILIES, called the Invocavit Sermons, stand with his brilliant performance at the Diet of Worms in importance in establishing and protecting his unique protest. The unrest of the autumn and the violence of the winter in Wittenberg forced him now to define his doctrine succinctly and powerfully.

Over his eight days of preaching Luther took on the issues one by one: the shape of the Mass, celibacy and monastic vows, images in the church, fasting, the sacrament, and confession. Yes,

The Invocavit Sermons. By Alexandre Struys. CREDIT: ULRICH KNEISE,
WARTBURG FOUNDATION

as Karlstadt had argued, when the Mass was performed as a sacrifice, it should be abolished, for in that way it was evil, and God
was displeased with it. Only when the Mass was evangelical was
it appropriate. The Word must be received freely from humble
preaching but never enforced as law. Nevertheless, its elimination had not been done in an "orderly way." Yes, the chalice
as well as the bread should be offered to the laity, but the practice should not be forced on the congregation. And indeed, if a
priest was not comfortable with chastity, he should get married,
and if a monk was troubled by the vows of obedience, chastity,

and poverty, he should, by all means, discard his robes. "For we cannot vow anything that is contrary to God's commands," Luther noted. But marriage for priests should not be obligatory, as Karlstadt had insisted; Luther's position was more nuanced. In his third sermon, he said, "Any monk who finds himself too weak to maintain chastity should conscientiously examine himself. If his heart and conscience are thus strengthened, let him take a wife and be a husband."

In his condemnation of images and icons, he was forceful. "It is far better to give a poor man a gold piece than God a golden image," he said. He did not like graven images and wished they were not in his church. But since the superstition about them was long-standing, "it is not by violence that they should be overturned. If the Devil had begged me to do it, I should have turned a deaf ear to him. But you rushed in, created an uproar, broke down altars and destroyed images. Do you really think you can abolish them that way? No, that way, you will only set them up more firmly." He reminded his audience of St. Paul in Athens when he went into the churches and condemned the icons as idolatrous. He did not destroy them but only preached against them in the marketplace. If the people were to find out that idols are worthless, they would disappear of their own accord.

Many people were weak in faith and invested in their time-worn rituals. They must be persuaded to new ways, not coerced. Patience and charity were his watchwords. He quoted his own translation of 1 Corinthians 13:1–2 to them: "If I speak in the tongues of men and of angels, but have not love, I am only a resounding gong or a clanging cymbal . . . and if I have faith so that I can move mountains and have no charity, I am nothing."

On the issue of the bread and wine, he told them a mouse could be a good Christian if the sacrament was only a question of eating and drinking. "True reception occurs in faith and is inward; otherwise it is nothing but sham and a mere external show." The Eucharist was only for the "hungering, longing man" who is battling his sins. Any who do not feel anxiety at coming to the table of the Lord should refrain from coming. But no one should be forced to take both bread and wine. "If you are going to follow me, stop it," he said in the fifth sermon to those who would compel the use of both kinds. "And if you are not going to follow me, I will leave you unasked, and I shall regret that I ever preached so much as a single sermon in this place."

This gentle, loving, but stern instruction to his flock represented his public posture. Even at the end of his eight days of preaching, he still bristled with anger at the violence that had been done to his movement in his absence. On March 17, the day after the last of his eight sermons, he wrote to a friendly evangelist in Zwickau: "The 'prophets' who came from your town are pregnant with monstrosities. If these should be endured, they will cause no small damage. Their spirit is extremely deceitful and specious." And then he vented his ire at the hypocrisy of the innovators: "Nothing is more disgusting to me than our mob of people here who have abandoned Word, faith, and love and can only boast that they are Christians because before the very eyes of the weak they can eat meat, eggs, and milk on fast days, receive the Lord's Supper in both kinds and neither fast nor pray."

The Invocavit Sermons were a triumph of oratory for their eloquence, their political power, and their encouragement of unity within a model congregation. Their upshot was the banishment of Luther's rivals and pretenders. Already banned from preaching, Karlstadt was brought before a university disciplinary board, censured, and driven from town. He ended up as a parish pastor in nearby Orlamünde, where he exchanged his university vestments for peasant attire and sought out the common folk for their wisdom. Gabriel Zwilling was more contrite, confessing his errors and agreeing never again to disparage the Eucharist with student vestments and a feather in his cap. He was dispatched to lowly duties in the town of Altenburg in Thuringia. And the students themselves returned to their classrooms.

The dispatch of his rivals had about it a certain irony, for on many of the finer points of their theology there was little difference between Luther and his opponents, especially Karlstadt. Like Luther, Karlstadt had advocated communion of both kinds, though Luther said no one should be forced to take both. Like Karlstadt he saw confession as unnecessary, though Luther did not want the practice abolished but only made voluntary. Like Karlstadt, Luther condemned the Mass when it was presented as a sacrifice, but the way Karlstadt had changed it was, to Luther, a disorderly act of force. Both had condemned celibacy, but Luther was against a general law about it, one way or another. Let a priest get married if he needed to relieve his conscience, he said. Karlstadt had violently destroyed icons and images in the church; Luther only wanted them peaceably removed.

Ultimately, the struggle between Luther and Karlstadt was as much about the pace of innovation, about personality and charisma, and about control, as it was about the direction of the reform movement. Their differences were over method not substance, and over the issue of whether compulsion or persuasion was most effective in obtaining the reforms they sought. On this point, Luther had the last word: "Christ did not seek the conversion of men by fire and sword."

And so in the eight days of preaching Martin Luther had triumphed in a critical power struggle and saved his movement. If his previous reputation was that of a rabble rouser, now he presented himself as a peacemaker and the avatar of social order, calming the turbulent waters of his beloved Wittenberg.

Seventeen

FRUITION

ONCE LUTHER SETTLED BACK INTO HIS ROLE AS THE principal preacher of Wittenberg, and the leader of a rapidly spreading continental movement, he turned his mind to bringing his great work at the Wartburg to fruition. He had brought home with him several hundred handwritten pages that constituted his work of translation. (He had mailed the first portion of his work on March 1.) At this stage, the pages had the look of chicken scratches, with lines crossed out and rewritten, arrows pointing hither and yon, smudges and blackouts. These had to be deciphered and cleaned up and made comprehensible for the eventual publisher. Now, at last, he was back in the company of friends and colleagues who could help.

Through the spring Luther and his chief assistants, George Spalatin and Philipp Melanchthon, concentrated on the task of correcting and editing, polishing and proofreading the manuscript. There was an abundance of facts to check. In Revelation 21, for example, the next to last chapter of the Bible, where the new heaven and new earth is mentioned and God proclaims himself to be the Alpha and the Omega, the walls of the new

Jerusalem are bejeweled with precious stones, which were not all identified in the Greek and Hebrew texts. So through the good offices of Lucas Cranach, Luther insisted on seeing the gems in the treasury of Elector Frederick to be sure he had the correct names and colors of jasper, sapphire, agate, emerald, onyx, carnelian, chrysolite, beryl, topaz, chrysoprase, jacinth, and amethyst.

Beyond the polish of the text itself, Luther decided that an introduction was necessary for the whole work and that each book as well should have its own introduction. Moreover, since this was to be a gift for the masses, Luther wanted brief notations to appear in the margins alongside difficult, obscure, or especially important passages of his Bible as a guide for understanding the finer points of the text.

Lucas Cranach was soon brought into the process. In Frederick's court painter Luther had not only his illustrator but also the chief officer of a business conglomerate that included a booming real estate enterprise; trade in Italian sweet wine, ink, paper, writing quills, print colors, and salt and pepper; and a full service pharmacy. Cranach was ecumenical in his business dealings. If he was to serve Luther as an anti-Catholic propagandist, he was also not above painting beautiful Madonnas for Luther's adversary, Archbishop Albrecht of Mainz, or lascivious Venuses for well-heeled voluptuaries.

Now the painter agreed to create a series of woodcuts to illustrate scenes from the Book of Revelation. In this challenge Cranach had before him the masterworks of Albrecht Dürer, whose amazing series of phantasmagoric woodcuts on the Apocalypse from 1498 included the Four Horsemen and the Whore of Babylon. For years Cranach had struggled to escape the shadow of his more famous rival from Nürnberg. Even in the affections of his prince, Elector Frederick, Cranach had to contend with the big feet of Dürer, since Frederick continued independently to commission Dürer for a number of works.

From a distance Dürer was himself a great admirer of Luther. In 1520 Spalatin, on behalf of the elector, had sent him a sample of Luther's writings, and the famous artist had replied: "If with God's help I could come to Martin Luther, I would paint him with diligence and engrave him on copper, as a lasting memorial to that Christian man who has helped me to overcome great fears." This last phrase applied to the crisis of conscience and spiritual doubt that Dürer himself was experiencing in this period. Thirsting for religious truth and clarity, he had found a measure of solace in the Reformation, though he steadfastly believed that reform could take place from within the church. For him the challenges of religious art were joined with the problems of belief.

In 1521 Dürer was in Antwerp, engaged in costume studies, when he learned of Luther's sensational performance at Worms. And then he was shocked to hear the erroneous rumor that after Worms Luther had been captured and killed.

"Whether he lives or whether they have murdered him, I do not know," Dürer wrote at the time. "But he has suffered in the cause of Christian truth. Ah, God in heaven! Have pity upon us. Pray for us, Lord Jesus Christ. Save us when our time shall come. . . . If Luther is dead who will expound to us so clearly the Holy Gospel? What might he not have written in twenty or thirty years! O all ye pious Christian men! Help me diligently to mourn this man inspired by God and pray to Him that He may send us another enlightened man!" Shortly after Dürer left Antwerp in July 1521, Luther's writings were publicly burned in accordance with the Edict of Worms under the watchful eye of Cardinal Girolamo Aleander, Luther's prosecutor at Worms.

Dürer would never get a chance to paint Luther, and he was not the only famous artist who longed to paint the Reformer. In 1522 in Basel, Switzerland, the German artist Hans Holbein the Younger was working on a painting of Luther as Hercules destroying the pillars of the Catholic Church. A year later Holbein designed an exquisite title page for a Swiss edition of Luther's New Testament.

But in Wittenberg during the initial production of the first New Testament, Cranach had the field to himself. In crafting his woodcuts of the Apocalypse for Luther's Bible, Cranach's challenge was how to separate himself stylistically from Dürer's 1498 series.

Within Cranach's workshop was also a publisher, Melchior Lotter, who hailed from Leipzig and whose father, a notable publisher as well, had printed Luther's Ninety-Five Theses five years earlier. Once Lotter set up his printing equipment in Cranach's establishment in 1520, his first publications had been Luther's three controversial books of advocacy, *To the Christian Nobility of the German Nation*, *The Babylonian Captivity of the Church*, and *The Freedom of a Christian*.

Now, as the production of the translation went forward, its existence remained a closely held secret. Only Melanchthon, Spalatin, Elector Frederick, Cranach, and Nicholas von Amsdorf, now the president of the university, knew about the project. With the publisher waiting in anticipation, there was an additional reason for secrecy: marketing. This was long before copyright was an accepted protection against literary theft, and there was a very real chance that, if word about the translation got out, some other enterprising publisher might try to get their hands on the manuscript and beat Lotter to market. Lotter wanted to launch the entire work with surprise and fanfare in late September at the bustling Leipzig Trade Fair. They now had a deadline to concentrate their attention. Illustrations by Cranach, Lotter knew, were certain to increase sales among the largely illiterate Germans.

Luther's herculean literary endeavor was well served by the newly modernized and professionalized publishing industry in Europe. In the centuries before Johann Gutenberg invented his printing press around 1440, copyists—usually monks in monasteries—produced the only Bibles, and the mistake-filled process could take more than a decade to finish a single copy. (Ironically, Gutenberg made most of his money initially by mass-producing indulgence sheets for the Catholic Church.)

Since Gutenberg's publication of the first printed Bible sixty-seven years earlier, the printing process had exploded across Europe. The first rudimentary screw presses with moveable type, inspired by wine and olive oil presses, had improved dramatically in the intervening years. The first color printing occurred in 1467 with an illustrated Psalter, and in 1476 copper engraving took its place alongside woodcuts for illustration. By the turn of the century the business of printing was booming in over several hundred towns of Europe, and it is believed that more than fifteen million printed books existed by Luther's time. Since the printing of his Ninety-Five Theses, Luther and his movement had benefited mightily from the ability of printers to turn out his tracts and books quickly. But this was different. The Luther Bible was a work of art—and almost surely a huge best seller in the making.

In the spring of 1522 work on the Bible proceeded quickly. The pages were designed in a single column rather than the double columns of previous Bibles, so that there would be room for Luther's marginalia. Elaborate decorated drop capitals began each chapter. At first, only one press was used, but eventually a second and third were added, as the anticipation of large sales became evident. On May 10 the first folios came off Lotter's press. By the early summer, the Gospels of Matthew, Mark, and Luke, as well as Paul's Epistles to the Romans and Corinthians, were completed. As the folios were printed and assembled, Luther worked on his introductions.

His introduction to the New Testament reflected the insights he had gained at the Wartburg and the lessons he had learned in his struggle with the radicals. But first he spoke to the multitude of his readers about the nature of the book itself. A testament was a bequeathal, and a Gospel was a good message that, if the reader believed it to be true, would make him laugh and rejoice and sing at the good news. "See to it," Luther wrote to his reader, "that you do not make of Christ a second Moses, or of the Gospel a book of laws and doctrines." For in these Gospels, he explained, Christ does not compel or command but invites and entreats, while the apostles only exhort and beg but do not decree. The only commandment in the New Testament, he wrote, is to love.

Inevitably, the core of his introduction was his doctrine of justification by faith alone. "If faith is there, the believer cannot hold himself back. He breaks out into good works," he wrote. "Everything for which he lives and does is directed to his neighbor's profit."

How then should the New Testament be read? Here Luther made some startling distinctions. John's Gospel, St. Paul's Epistles (especially to the Romans), and St. Peter's Epistle were the "true kernel and marrow of all the books." Indeed, John's Gospel, he asserted, is the chief Gospel, far superior to the other three. For John writes little about Christ's works but much about His preaching, while the other three books are about works and little about Christ's preaching. Luther preferred the preaching, "for works do not help me, but His words give life." As he had concluded at the Wartburg, the Epistle of St. James was worthless. The reader should forget about it.

Curiously, the one book of the New Testament about which Luther had his gravest doubts was chosen to be the sole place to receive Cranach's illustrations. As Cranach carved his wood in his workshop, Luther wrote his damning introduction to the Book of Revelation. Nowhere in it could he find evidence that the Holy Spirit had produced it. Nowhere in it was Christ mentioned; therefore, it was not apostolic, for the job of the apostle was to witness Christ. Nor was it prophetic. "I cannot fit my spirit into this book," he wrote. "Therefore, I stick to the books that give me Christ clearly and purely." Luther left it to the reader to make of the book what he or she would.

It was left to the visuals to pack the wallop. Cranach's woodcuts were scarcely neutral. The most famous of his twenty-one illustrations adapted the ponderous biblical fantasies of Revelation to anti-papal and anti-Rome propaganda. For the wild story of the Whore of Babylon (Revelation 17:1–8), with whom the kings of the earth are said to have committed fornication and who emerges from the deep astride a monster with seven heads and ten horns, Cranach fashioned a woman with a coquettish, sidelong glance, appearing slightly drunk as she holds a golden cup "full of the abomination and filthiness of her fornication." Upon her head rests, slightly askew, a papal tiara.

With Revelation 14:8 Cranach was equally pointed in his anti-Vatican perspective. This verse of scripture announces the fall of Babylon: the once-great city collapses into a den of Devils, holding "every foul spirit" and "every unclean and hateful bird" (18:2), because, as Luther translated the verse, she has impregnated all nations with the wine of her ferocious fornication. No doubt with Luther's approval, Cranach made Babylon into Rome. The broken, crenellated towers and palaces of Cranach's woodcut bore the unmistakable Roman imprint.

Cranach's depictions of the last days before the advent of the New Jerusalem are ghoulish, terrifying, and mesmerizing, replete with multiheaded dragons, insects with human faces, cowering humans in the bottomless pit, dreadful angels pouring out the vials of wrath, and cataclysms as the seven seals are opened, announced with trumpet blasts and falling stars. It is no wonder that Luther was uninterested in trying to make sense of the

Whore of Babylon with papal tiara. By Lucas Cranach the Elder.

fantastic scenes. But Cranach resurrected their power, making the inscrutable stories exciting and frightening and commercially appealing.

The *Septembertestament*, as Luther's first edition of his New Testament translation was to be called, was meant for a mass audience. Printed on paper handmade from cloth rags, measuring six and a half inches by eleven and a half inches, and two inches thick, with 444 pages, it was intended as a family Bible. (A year later a pocket-sized edition, four inches by six inches, was published.) Because a large sector of the target audience was illiterate, the Cranach woodcuts provided the first attraction for the casual buyer. Their visual appeal, along with their sheer evocativeness, made them a hugely effective propaganda tool in Luther's struggle with the Catholic Church.

It has been said Luther was the first to employ visual caricature as a political weapon, and Cranach's images would arouse more passionate umbrage among Catholic commentators than any other part of the translation. They would be dubbed Cranach's "cartoons." No one could dispute their appeal and their effectiveness. To the traditionalists, they were vulgar, coarse, venomous slander, intended to ridicule the church and thereby to engender hatred and contempt for it.

Their sting was still evident four hundred years later. In an analysis by Francis Betten, an early-twentieth-century Jesuit writer, one can feel the hurt: "As long as the ridiculing of an adversary keeps to the truth, it may be permissible, but even then only within certain rather narrow limits. If it is based on distortions of truth, on misrepresentations and positive lies, and if besides it transgresses the bounds of decency and even modesty, it is the more criminal the more it is apt to mislead the uneducated and the thoughtless. It must be deplored as an onslaught on right thinking, on charity, and on civilization in general."

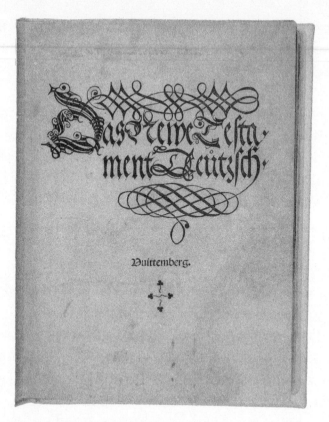

Title page of the Luther's Septembertestament.
By Lucas Cranach the Elder. CREDIT: PEABODY
LIBRARY, BALTIMORE

A S THE START OF THE LEIPZIG TRADE FAIR ON SEPTEMBER 29
drew closer, Lotter, Luther, and their teams worked frantically to complete the printing in time. On September 20 Luther
wrote to Spalatin that the book was nearly finished, except for
his preface to Paul's Epistle to the Romans. He finished it overnight and on the following day sent it to the printer.

Finally, the book was ready. The first recipient was appropri-
ately Elector Frederick, who got three copies. But Luther wanted

to honor the person to whom he felt most indebted, dispatching a copy sentimentally to the Wartburg and to Hans von Berlepsch, his captain and protector, as a token of gratitude and affection. In the fullness of his generosity, Lotter allowed Luther to take one copy for himself, and Luther took no payment for his work. How many of the initial printing of three thousand copies Lotter loaded on his wagon to take to Leipzig is not known. The unbound sheets were packed into barrels for transport. As with most books sold at that time, the binding would be left to the customer.

The Leipzig Trade Fair was at the crossroads of central Europe, where hides and skins came in bulk from Russia in the east and where fish products came from the North Sea south to Nürnberg and Augsburg. It had been in existence for over 350 years, and it was the premier commercial exposition of all Germany. Only 15 years earlier, Emperor Maximilian I, the predecessor of Charles V, had conferred imperial status on the exposition, downgrading the importance of smaller trade fairs in surrounding cities like Halle, Erfurt, and Magdeburg. Tradesmen converged on the town for the one-week extravaganza from all points on the compass. Lucas Cranach visited the fair regularly, for art as well as books was traded and commissioned there.

Leipzig was then a dirty, smelly town of about eight thousand inhabitants. With cobblestone streets, its inner city was made up of well-built three-story stone houses, while its commercial area was centered in the market square next to the grand thirteenth-century Pleissenburg Castle. The success of the fair was largely due to the infrastructure that supported it. Apartments were provided for the visiting merchants, chambers for their helpers, and ample storage space for their wares. In the seedy suburbs outside the town were plenty of brothels, which housed about twelve prostitutes each, all of whom were supposed to be from the hinterland and not from Leipzig.

The town was also the publishing capital of Germany. In the first four decades of the sixteenth century some 1,800 books were published in Leipzig, ranging across the fields of law and philosophy, religion and philology. Melchior Lotter the Elder, the father of Luther's Wittenberg publisher, was one of the most renowned Leipzig publishers. Before 1520 the patriarch had published no fewer than forty-seven Luther tracts, and Luther had stayed in the Lotter household when he visited in 1519 to give the first evangelical sermon in the Pleissenburg Castle chapel. Now Lotter the Younger joined his father for the 1522 fair and set up his stall in competition with the purveyors of cloth, herring, pepper, and wine. The Lotters put Luther's Bible on sale for half a gulden, the equivalent price for ten pounds of butter or one week's pay for a skilled carpenter. Despite this steep price, the first edition of the *Septembertestament* sold out quickly.

In all the hustle and bustle, Duke George of Saxony would scarcely notice the arrival of this subversive tome in his fiercely Catholic domain. But when the duke finally got wind of it, he put out the word that he would buy any copy for the going price, and then he burned his haul.

But Luther's movement and all its works was now far beyond the control of a mere provincial duke of Saxony.

WHEN COPIES OF LUTHER'S NEW TESTAMENT REACHED Rome, the reaction to its textual alterations was swift and virulent. His translation of Romans 3:23–24 was especially repellent. Catholic scholars pointed out that Paul used the word "faith" more than two hundred times in his Epistles but never coupled it with the word "alone." The sacrament of penance was central to the Catholic view of justification, but of course Luther denied that penance was a sacrament at all. When the furor in Rome over the word "alone" came to Luther's notice some time later, he scoffed. "I would like to see a papist come forward and translate into German one epistle of St. Paul without making use of Luther's German," he was to write. His papal detractors were braying donkeys, blockheads, scribblers, brazen idiots. They stared at the letters s-o-l-a (in *sola fide*) like "cows at a new gate."

Twenty-five years later, over fierce political objection, the doctrine of justification became a major topic at the Council of Trent, as Luther lay dying in the town of his birth at Eisleben. The Catholic prelates debated the issue for months and ultimately found agreement in this proclamation: "the believer is justified by the good works he performs by the grace of God and the merit of Jesus Christ." In short, good works purified and perfected faith, and the combination of the two led to salvation. More sharply, the council banned from the church any who argued that by faith alone the impious sinner is justified. And it reaffirmed that the Vulgate of St. Jerome was the authorized text of the Bible.

To bolster their argument, the participants in the Council of Trent invoked a passage from the Epistle of James (James 2:17, 24): "Faith without works is dead, being alone. . . . By works man is justified and not by faith alone." Of course, Luther had famously proclaimed the Epistle of James to be "an epistle of straw." There was, he felt, a fundamental contradiction between Paul and James, and he would later say that he would give his doctor's beret to any theologian who could reconcile the two Epistles.

The labor on Luther's New Testament translation did not cease with its first publication in September 1522. Because the first edition sold so quickly, a second edition was in the works within days of Melchior Lotter the Younger's trip to the Leipzig Trade Fair. Luther and Melanchthon set immediately to work on corrections. There would be 574 of them when the second edition appeared in December of that year. Called the *Decembertestament,* its most notable change was an alteration of Cranach's scandalous image of the Whore of Babylon with the papal tiara cocked on her head like a cabaret dancer. That woodcut had prompted a firestorm of protest, and as a result Luther and Cranach relented, replacing the tiara with a goofy crown. The concession did not mollify Duke George of Saxony.

Within two years of its first publication fourteen more editions of the New Testament were published, along with sixty-six pirated editions. Luther, Melanchthon, and company then harnessed their energies toward the longer and more complicated translation of the Old Testament, with the oldest available Hebrew manuscripts as the primary source. This was a more difficult and tedious process. Melanchthon was a stickler for precision. "Sometimes it would take two weeks to get a single sentence correct," Melanchthon wrote later.

The printing process was not without its hitches. The younger Melchior Lotter got himself into trouble with the authorities after he tortured one of his helpers with a binder's needle and was forced to leave town. He was replaced with a publisher named Hans Lufft. But that randy fellow ran afoul of the authorities for "laying hands" on the good women of Wittenberg and was forced to pay the hefty fine of fifty gulden.

As the books of the Old Testament were finished, they were printed and released in a kind of serialization. The first five books of the Old Testament, the Pentateuch, were released in 1523; the second tranche came a year later with the books from Joshua to Esther; the third part, the poetic books of Job, Psalms, Proverbs, Ecclesiastes, and the Song of Solomon, came in 1524; between 1526 and 1530 the five books of the prophets were released individually. As before, Cranach's illustrations propelled the sales of the book into the stratosphere. By 1533 it was estimated that every tenth household in Germany owned a Luther Bible.

The full Luther Bible with both testaments was finally released in 1534, and it contained sixty-two Cranach illustrations. With the Old Testament as with the New, Luther made distinctions between books that constituted the Holy Writ and lesser books that were not entitled to such high distinction. These so-called deuterocanonical books, like Judith, Wisdom, and 1 and 2 Maccabees, he downgraded and put in an Apocrypha between the Old and New Testaments. (The word "apocrypha" means a collection of books whose authenticity as inspired writings is not admitted, and is therefore not to be considered part of the canon of Holy Scripture.)

The language of Luther's Bible, like the fresh ideas it contained, would prove to have a lasting impact. In due course certain phrases and poetic constructions from his translation made their way into the standard German language. *Seine Hände in Unschuld waschen*, literally "to wash one's hands in innocence," came to mean denying guilt and pretending to be innocent. *Ein Herz und eine Seele sein*, "to be one heart and one soul," meant to have a very strong relationship either in friendship or in love. *Jemandem sein Herz ausschütten*, "to pour one's heart out to someone," meant to share one's worries. *Sein Licht nicht unter den Scheffel stellen*, "don't put your light under the bushel," meant one should not be too modest. *Morgenland*, "morning land," meant the Orient; *Fallstrick*, "falling rope," meant a snare, trap, or pitfall; and *Machtwort*, "word of power," meant a decision by a person in authority, to be accepted without qualm.

THE NUMBER OF VERSIONS OF LUTHER'S BIBLE THAT WERE ultimately sold is nothing short of amazing, and it testifies to the power of both his translation and its message. By the time of Luther's death in 1546, there were 350 editions of his Bible. He had become, by far, the most published writer in the world.

Of these many editions and the offshoots of his Bible that spread far beyond Germany none is more important than William Tyndale's derivative translation into English. Educated at Oxford and Cambridge, Tyndale was an English Catholic priest who decided, not long after Luther returned from the Wartburg, to follow his idol's lead in bringing the Bible to "the English plough-boy." At this endeavor his superiors balked, and Tyndale fled to Europe to continue his work. In 1524 he visited Luther in Wittenberg and then settled in Cologne. There too the clerical police discovered his incendiary scheme and got the local authorities to interdict any printing. Not only that: word was sent to Henry VIII and Cardinal Wolsey to watch the English ports for the banned material. Tyndale slipped away to Worms, where his entire translation was first printed in 1526, and its pages were smuggled into England.

Like Luther's, Tyndale's style was noteworthy for its clarity and intensity, and over the years his accomplishment would be recognized and admired. Also like Luther Tyndale brought a number of poetic phrases into his native tongue: "When I was a child, I spake like a child. I thought like a child. I reasoned like a child. When I became a man, I gave up childish ways" (1 Corinthians 13:11). "Eat, drink, and be merry" (Luke 12:19). "Our Father which are in heaven, hallowed be thy name . . . " (Matthew 6:9–13).

But now he was a hunted man. In 1536 he was betrayed in Antwerp, tried, and strangled at the stake, before his body was burned. His Luther-influenced translation lived on, however, and grew in reputation. It was to become the primary source for the Jacobean translators of the King James Bible in the early seventeenth century. Some 94 percent of the New Testament in the King James edition was copied from Tyndale, who in turn had patterned his translation on Luther's.

EPILOGUE

MARTIN LUTHER WAS THIRTY-SEVEN YEARS OLD WHEN HE crafted his literary masterpiece at the Wartburg. In the twenty-four years he had yet to live, there would be many more crises and, from the Catholic point of view, many more scandals he had yet to foist on the world. Yet in this culmination of four turbulent years—his Ninety-Five Theses, his confrontations with Rome, his disputations with leading theologians, his excommunication by Rome and ban at the Diet of Worms, his exile at the Wartburg, and the consolidation of his movement with his Lenten sermons—his fame was continental, his doctrine was formulated, and his movement was well-rooted. In the crucible of Worms, the Wartburg, and Wittenberg during this time, his legacy was forged.

The first of these subsequent crises came in 1524–1525 with the violent events known as the Peasants' War or the Peasants' Revolt. The common people, to whom he had dedicated his biblical translation, remembered that Luther had called the coterie of Charles V a "sack of maggots" and the emperor himself a tyrant. He had referred to the princes of Germany as "mad, foolish, senseless, raving, frantic, and lunatic." He had prayed to God that the German nation would be delivered from them: "The princes know of nothing but flaying and squeezing and putting one tax upon the other, one rate upon the other. Here they send out a bear and there a wolf. No justice, no fidelity, no truth is to be found in them. They act in a manner that would be too much for robbers and knaves. There are few princes who are not considered fools and knaves. In the long run people will not and cannot stand their tyranny and their arbitrary proceedings. The world is not now what it used to be, when you drove and hunted such people as beasts."

With these words ringing in their ears, peasants rose in revolt all over Germany and Austria. Their rallying cry for greater economic and religious equality was "*Bundschuh! Bundschuh!*" a reference to the peasant's shoe that would flatten sacred and profane authority. Poorly armed and badly led, they were brutally crushed in one place, only to rise elsewhere with a violence equal to their oppressors—and then crushed again.

Luther found himself in the middle of the revolt. While he despised the nobles against whom the peasants were fighting, he valued social order. At first he beseeched the nobles to stop their violence and deal reasonably with the peasants. And he told the peasants that their revolt was taking the Lord's name in vain. As the butchery and arson continued—in Thuringen alone seventy monasteries were torched; in Franconia 293 castles were burned—he lost sympathy with the rebels altogether and swung over to the side of their oppressors.

He did so with a brutality of language that was remarkable for a man of the cloth, especially one who had helped to inspire the rebellion in the first place. His condemnations became increasingly apocalyptic: "Remember that rebellion is irreparable, and the destruction of the world may be expected at any hour." He associated "robbing, murdering peasants" with the Devil himself. They were guilty of every sin and "clothed their sins with the pretense of God's law. Let the nobles take the sword as ministers of God's wrath. Let him who can, stab, smite and destroy. If you fall, well it is for you. You could never die a happier death. Whosoever has it in his power to punish and spares the rod is guilty of all the slaughter that he does not prevent. Let there be no pity. It is the time of wrath not of mercy."

There was nothing more diabolical than a rebel, the rebel himself proclaimed, and no one seemed to remark upon the irony. "If you kill him, it is like killing a mad dog," Luther growled. "If you do not kill him, he will kill you and a whole country with you."

Amazingly for one who had presented himself as a peacemaker upon his return from the Wartburg, he conceded that the blood of the peasants was on his own head. "But I put it all on our Lord God, for he commanded me."

There was a lot of blood to take responsibility for in the suppression of the Peasants' Revolt. Tens of thousands died—men who had been inspired by Luther's "evangelical liberty" and who were dismayed by his betrayal. Included in the dead were scores of Lutheran ministers, who were hanged in Austria with the approval of Ferdinand I, the archduke of Austria and brother of Charles V. Instead of his famous conscience being troubled, Luther responded with self-serving grandiosity, prating about the peril that he imagined himself to be suffering: "I see clearly that the Devil who has been unable to murder me through the Pope, is now trying to destroy and devour me through bloodthirsty prophets and spirits among you. Well, let him devour me. His belly will get narrow enough then, I fancy."

Among the casualties of the Peasants' War was the Zwickau prophet Thomas Müntzer. At the Battle of Frankenhausen in May 1525 he led a horde of eight thousand peasants in battle, assuring his ragtag followers that God would surely intervene in their behalf the way He had done so five hundred years earlier at Santiago de Compostella. Instead, Müntzer's mob was routed; the Anabaptist hero was captured, imprisoned, and tortured. Under this rigorous examination, as torture was then called, he recanted his views about divine revelation before he was beheaded in Mühlhausen, in the province of Thuringen. When he heard about it, Luther claimed Müntzer's death was God's punishment.

Eventually, the peasant movement burned itself out. The farmers returned to their fields with little to show for their uprising, as the old order reasserted itself in a harsher form. It was not Luther's finest hour, and he was widely criticized as a flatterer of princes. But his inconsistency and betrayal did not tamp down the ardor for his brand of worship. The contagion of Luther's rebellion now had a life of its own and was impervious to the bluster and contradictions of its founder.

I N LATE 1522, AFTER HIS RETURN FROM THE WARTBURG, Luther had addressed marriage directly in a sermon called "Increase and Multiply," taking his text from Genesis 1:28: "God blessed them, and God said unto them, Be fruitful, and multiply, and replenish the earth." "As little as we can do without eating and drinking, just as impossible is it to abstain from women," he told his Wittenberg congregation. "The reason is that we have been conceived and nourished in a woman's womb. Of women we are born and begotten. Hence our own flesh is for the most part woman's flesh, and it is impossible to keep away from it. Chastity is not in our power. He who resolves to remain single let him give up the name of human being. Let him prove that he is an angel or a spirit." As if these thoughts on chastity were not shocking enough, he uttered the phrase that would be most remembered of all in the sermon. On the subject of conjugal relations and divorce, he said,

"If the wife refuses, let the servant maid come."

In early 1523 twelve apostate Cistercian nuns, most of them from noble families, escaped the rigors of their Nimbischen convent on a Good Friday by hiding in empty herring barrels. Nine of them made their way to Wittenberg, where they were sequestered by Luther and his colleagues. Luther's writings had inspired them, and it eventually came out that Luther himself had planned their escape. Soon after, in April 1523, Luther published a tract entitled "Why Virgins May Leave Convents with Divine Sanction." Among the runaway nuns was Katharina von Bora, who came from a family of landed gentry.

On June 13, 1525, in a private ceremony in Wittenberg with Lucas Cranach as a witness, Luther married her. Given its high visibility, his marriage was an extraordinarily provocative act, and it was done not out of love initially but rather as an expression of inward completion, as relief for the guilt he felt as a monk over sexual temptation, and as a natural consequence of his thought.

His marriage caused a great sensation. Catholics considered his betrothal to be a sacrilege and heresy committed by his own body. Not only that. As monk and nun, Luther and Katharina were engaging in incest, the Roman church believed, since their vows assumed that each was betrothed to Christ. "If the monk marries," said an opponent, "the whole world and the Devil will laugh, and he himself will destroy everything he has done."

Luther responded to the criticism characteristically. His marriage song came from the seventh chapter of Paul's First Epistle to the Corinthians: "To avoid fornication, let every man have his own wife, and let every woman have her own husband" (1 Corinthians 7:2). To him now marriage was more than sex. It led to salvation. If the world was not scandalized, he said grandly, he would be afraid that his work was not divine. It was as if he were again channeling his relation to Jesus. "Where Christ is, he always goes against the flow." Where Luther was, it seemed, it was the same. He would have six children by Katharina von Bora, and the family would take over the Black Cloister, the former Augustinian monastery in Wittenberg, as its home.

AFTER THE WARTBURG, THE SUCCESS OF LUTHER'S MOVEMENT no longer depended on the abrasive statements and bon mots of its founder. Lutheranism was sweeping across Europe on the shoulders of Lutheran precepts. Its popularity came from its emphasis on the interior life of the Christian in contrast to the exterior trappings of Roman Catholicism. The emphasis on spiritual liberty and on perfect love was seductive, as was the abolition of burdens like confession, alms, offerings, fasting, and obedience to church hierarchy. Simple churches without icons and decoration were appealing. Most of all, justification by faith alone captured the public mind, relaxed the focus on good works, and placed the emphasis on the inner spiritual life of the believer.

In contrast to the radicals, Luther encouraged changes in the Mass and in liturgy to be gradual and almost imperceptible, so as not to shock his followers. He continued to preach in his Augustinian cowl until 1524, when he discarded it in favor of a simple burgher's coat. So many Catholic priests left the Catholic faith and descended on Wittenberg to become Lutheran ministers that Luther remarked, "Who can deliver us from these hordes?"

The political situation in Europe after the Wartburg, meanwhile, redounded mightily to the benefit of Lutheranism. Charles V had decamped immediately from the Diet of Worms to Italy, where for the next seven years he was consumed by the war against Francis I and France in northern Italy. The papacy was caught between the two sides, vacillating one way and then another, with the dominion of the papal states constantly in peril. Of Leo X's foreign policy before he died, it was said that he played the game with two hands at once.

The woeful papacy of Adrian VI followed that of Leo and, unintentionally, gave Lutheranism still more time to take hold. After Adrian's election in January 1522, it took a number of weeks before an official delegation of legates could even be empanelled to travel to Spain and escort the holy father to Rome. Once organized, the delegation took with it the demand that the new pope do all in his power to extirpate heresy in Germany. But this would prove to be an empty demand.

Once the escorts finally arrived in Tortosa, Adrian found reasons to delay his trip further. How would he travel to Rome? Overland through France was out of the question for political reasons (although the pope-elect had already signaled that he would not be part of an anti-French league). By ship along the coastline was highly risky because of the presence of Turkish pirates in the Ligurian and Tyrrhenian Seas. In the end the sea route was chosen, but a flotilla of fifty ships was deemed to be necessary for protection, and it would take time to mobilize the armada. Meanwhile, during this interregnum, warring parties inside and outside the Vatican continued their squabbling. The discord between French and imperial cardinals continued unabated. Rumors circulated in Rome that the new pope was already dead, causing further confusion.

When the "barbarian" pope finally arrived in the Eternal City in late August 1522, Rome knew immediately that a new era had arrived. Adrian's physical appearance was in sharp contrast to the obese and jolly Leo. His face was long and pale, his body lean, his demeanor pious and serious. "I love poverty," he proclaimed to the beggars outside the Vatican walls. "You will see what I can do for you."

He spoke no Italian and proceeded to conduct all business in Latin. Patronizing Leo's cardinals as schoolboys, he evicted them from their plush Vatican apartments and commanded them to shave their beards and act like priests rather than potentates. Leo's resident musicians and poets were sent packing, along with Raphael's pupils. The subjects of Renaissance artists were to the new pope akin to paganism. Instead of taking charge of the glorious papal apartments, now luminous with Raphael's masterworks, he announced that he would live in a small house in the Vatican gardens, attended not by the legion of retainers who served Leo but by four persons, including an aging Flemish woman who cooked his simple meals.

Further diverting the attention of the Vatican from the German scandals was a new visitation of the plague. It came to Rome that summer, just as the new pope finally arrived from Spain. The grandees of the city fled to the countryside in droves, along with the Italian officials, and the business of the city largely ground to a halt. Adrian was urged to flee as well. As the bodies piled up in the streets, the pope proclaimed his intention to remain in place. "I have no fear for myself. I put my trust in God," he said. As the pestilence persisted into the late fall, Baldassare Castiglione wrote: "Eight out of ten persons whom one meets bear marks of the plague. Only a few men have survived. I fear lest God should annihilate the inhabitants of this city. The greatest mortality has been among grave-diggers, priests, and physicians. Where the dead have no relatives, it is hardly any longer possible to give them burial." The pope issued a decree against the sale of the dead persons' belongings.

When the plague finally receded with the cool weather of December, war remained the most pressing issue for Adrian. Fighting continued to rage in northern Italy, in Eastern Europe, and most urgently on the island of Rhodes, where the valiant

Knights of St. John were bracing for an invasion by the over-whelming forces of the infidel Ottoman sultan, Suleyman the Magnificent. The epidemic of Lutheranism stayed in the back-ground. It was not until January 1523, thirteen months after the death of Leo X, that Adrian finally addressed the Luther issue formally. Pushing for the enforcement of the Edict of Worms, he spoke sadly of the division that now visited "our once so steadfast German nation."

"We cannot think of anything so incredible as that so pious a union should allow a petty monk, an apostate from that Catholic faith which for years he had preached, to seduce it from the way pointed by the Savior and His Apostles, sealed by the blood of so many martyrs, trodden by so many wise and holy men," he wrote. He called on all good Christians to quench this fire and bring Lu-ther back into the "right way" by any means in their power. But if the villain would not listen, then the "rod of severity" had to be employed. "If the evil has penetrated so far that gentle means of healing are of no avail, then we must have recourse to methods of severity in order to safeguard the members as yet untainted by disease."

If the menace and the danger were clearly present in this pa-pal declaration, especially coming from the former head of the Spanish Inquisition, it came too late to have much effect on the spread of Lutheranism. The concatenation of events—Leo's death, the dysfunctional election of his successor, the antipathy and even contempt for the outsider, Adrian's long delay in get-ting to Rome, the plague, and the crisis in Rhodes—took the pressure off Luther and provided him with breathing space to consolidate his movement. By the time of the papal declaration of January 1523, Luther had finished his translation of the Bible, had left the Wartburg, and was back in Wittenberg, riding high in relative safety.

But something even more important than all these factors was brewing. Adrian VI came to Rome determined to address the abuses of the church and reform the Curia. In his first weeks he took steps to end the sale of ecclesiastical offices to unworthy persons for exorbitant prices, to quash the luxurious lifestyle of cardinals, and to reduce the bloated papal establishment. He deplored the simony, the nepotism, and the pluralism of the Vatican. He invoked St. Bernard, who had spoken of evil reaching such a fever pitch that the sinful could no longer smell the stench of their sins. And most significantly, he was prepared to stop the indiscriminate abuse of indulgences. Indulgences encouraged sin. Adrian's focus on the church's internal abuses was implicitly a validation of Luther's revolt against Rome.

Moreover, sentiment was growing that the time for severe measures against the Lutheran rebels had passed. Perhaps even an amnesty coupled with an emphasis on Vatican abuses was in order. Talk of roasting Luther in the holy fire should cease; reaching out to the rebel in sincere brotherly conciliation was the better course. It was universally recognized that a popular uprising in Germany was the nightmare to be avoided at all costs. Such a disaster would surely be the result of any attempt to seize Luther and suppress his movement. Even Erasmus of Rotterdam was counseling conciliation. And Cardinal Aleander, the man who had interrogated Luther at Worms, made the connection between the corruption of the Vatican and the Lutheran revolt.

"Let the Pope and the Curia do away with their errors by which God and man are justly offended," he said. "Let them bring the clergy once more under discipline. If the Germans see this done, there will be no further talk of Luther. The root and the cure of the evil are in ourselves."

Still the pontiff's efforts at reform spread consternation through certain sectors of the Vatican. The mood of the city changed quickly from anticipation to repugnance for the new pope and resistance to his harsh, ham-handed methods. As the fall proceeded, Adrian turned out to be reclusive and just as indecisive as Leo X. "When he does consent to see anyone," wrote the Venetian ambassador, "he says little and cannot make up his mind. Whatever the request, big or small, his answer is always the same: 'We shall see.'"

The goals that Adrian had set for himself at the beginning of his papacy faded rapidly. On Christmas Day, 1522, the bastion of Rhodes fell to the Muslim forces of Suleyman the Magnificent. At the news Adrian wept at the disarray of the Christian nations he had been unable to unite against the infidel. "Woe to Princes who do not employ the sovereignty conferred upon them by God, but abuse it in internecine strife," he wrote to the king of Portugal. And in Germany heresy was rife and burgeoning. The story spread that on the very day Rhodes fell, a piece of marble molding over the door of the pope's chapel fell and killed a papal guard, just as the pope was entering to pray. This was widely interpreted as a sign of God's wrath at the inability of the pope to protect the true religion.

Still, while the papacy of Adrian VI was brief and notable only for its failure, he became the first pope to acknowledge the abuse and corruption of the church. In calling for major reform, he said, "We all, prelates and clergy, have gone astray from the right way. For long there is not one who has done good, no, not one." This admission of collective guilt was roundly rejected by the entrenched ecclesiastics, who howled that such a sentiment undercut the case of the church against Luther. But Adrian was undaunted. "When the Savior wished to cleanse the city of Jerusalem of its sickness, he went first to the Temple to punish the sins of the priests," he proclaimed. "We know well that for many years things deserving abhorrence have gathered around the

Holy See. Sacred things have been misused, ordinances trans-
gressed. Therefore, we must promise to use all diligence to reform
the Roman Curia."

Luther could not have said it better.

Adrian's forthright admission of the Vatican's role in Luther's
rise to power marked the first, tiny step toward counter-
reformation. That revival of Roman Catholicism, prodded by
the Protestant Reformation, would begin twenty-three years later
with the Council of Trent at about the time of Luther's death and
continue for another hundred years.

AFTER ADRIAN'S FAILED PAPACY OF TWENTY MONTHS, LEO X'S
nephew became pope in November 1523 and took the
name Clement VII. He announced tepidly that he would enforce the Edict of Worms "as far as it was possible"—which was
not at all. All efforts to forge an anti-Lutheran alliance among
the princes of Germany failed. In 1527 Clement would have the
unpleasant experience of witnessing the sack of Rome, an event
whose main perpetrators were German Protestants and which is
often cited as the end of the Renaissance.

Meanwhile, external threats to Christendom were also growing rapidly. Ferdinand I of Austria had nominal sway over Saxony, but the newly ascendant Ottoman Empire under its vibrant
young sultan, Suleyman the Magnificent, threatened Vienna
with a massive army of hundreds of thousands. Suleyman was
encroaching farther and farther north through the Balkans and
endangered the heart of Europe as he announced his intention
to make Europe Islamic all the way to the Rhine River. Twice, in
1529 and 1532, the Turkish juggernaut stood before the gates of
Vienna, only to falter and pull back.

Closer to Lutheranism's epicenter, Duke George the Bearded
continued to spearhead bitter opposition to the Protestant revolt.

In 1523 he had banned all of Luther's works, including his Bible, and in 1525 two men were hanged in Leipzig for distributing Lutheran literature. But the duke was impoverished, and his efforts at suppression were ineffective, as Reformation printers simply moved their operations away from Leipzig and its trade fair. Duke George ruled until 1539, and after that his strictures were relaxed.

Elector Frederick the Wise died on May 5, 1525. On his deathbed he asked to receive the Eucharist in both kinds as a sign that he had finally become a Lutheran. Luther hastened to his bedside but arrived too late. For all their dealings together, the Reformer had never met his most stalwart, important protector in person.

After the Wartburg experience, Luther's literary output continued to be prodigious, as he underscored and fine-tuned his essential message. As he grew comfortable, and his body expanded into the pudgy figure that is the most familiar to a modern audience, he would repair almost nightly to the Black Eagle to imbibe and converse with his inner circle, often including his wife.

"He who drinks much beer sleeps well," he told his friends. "He who sleeps well does not sin. And he who does not sin goes to heaven."

Occasionally, the talk was coarse, but more often it was witty and instructive. Sometimes tempers flared, and Luther the peacemaker would quiet the scene by saying, "Let minds clash, but keep the fists down." This "table talk" was recorded by his disciples and has come down through the ages in multiple volumes. Toward the end of Luther's life, a participant would write: "Although our doctor often took weighty and profound thoughts to table with him and sometimes maintained the silence of the monastery during the entire meal, yet at times he spoke in a very jovial way. We used to call his conversation the condiments of the meal because we preferred it to all the spices and dainty food."

In the year after he returned from the Wartburg, Luther began to compose music with the same intensity with which he composed his essays and sermons. Music had been important to him from his early life, extending back to his choir boy days in Eisenach. It was one of four required study areas for all the boys, along with arithmetic, geometry, and astronomy. When as a teenager he injured himself with a sword, he learned to play the lute and continued with the instrument throughout his life. To sing lustily cheered his soul and his spirit and, as he would say later, relieved his temptations and his melancholy. He had long appreciated the value of music to move his listeners, to propagate his faith, and to spread the gospel to his illiterate followers.

Collaborating with a musician on the melodies, he supplied the powerful lyrics. His first Christmas composition, "*Gelobet seist du, Jesu Christ*" ("Praise to You, Jesus Christ"), used the melody from an old church song from 1460. The melody for his first original hymn, "*Nun freut euch, lieben Christen g'mein*" ("Now Christians one and all, rejoice . . . and proclaim the wonder God has done"), was completed in 1523, using the score of an old drinking song. This raised eyebrows, but Luther asked unapologetically, How else were people to remember his songs?

Some of his lyrics were overtly political. One hymn focused on the execution of two Lutherans in Belgium. Another, written expressly for children, was directed against all his arch-enemies, from the pope to the infidel Turks. But the most remembered are the defiant fight songs of the Reformation: "*Wach auf, wach auf, du deutsches Land*"—"Wake up, wake up, you German land. Think what God gave you, for which he created you"—and, of course, his stirring, bombastic "A Mighty Fortress Is Our God." It was printed in the first Protestant hymn book, published in 1524, along with twenty-three other hymns. The intensity of Luther's experience at the Wartburg surely gave extra meaning to the

Musical score: A Mighty Fortress is Our God. CREDIT: STIFTUNG
LUTHERGEDENKSTÄTTEN IN SACHSEN-ANHALT, WITTENBERG

words of his heroic Reformation anthem. It was inspired by Psalm
46, which Luther had translated as: "God is our comfort and our
strength, a help in great emergency which we have met." Later,
Johann Sebastian Bach was to arrange the anthem multiple times
in his chorales, imparting to it a chiseled harmonic structure. Its
powerful notes and bold, muscular lines—every line is a state-
ment ending with an exclamation point—were picked up var-
iously by such composers as George Frederick Handel, Richard
Wagner, and Claude Debussy. Felix Mendelssohn made it the
central motive in the fourth movement of his Symphony Number 5, known as his Reformation Symphony.

The Wartburg had been a mighty fortress for Luther, and
his time there a bulwark against his fears and temptations and

self-doubt. In his silence and solitude he had confronted the craft and power of the Prince of Darkness and learned through his own inner strength not to fear him. The world had threatened to undo his movement, but he had triumphed. The last words of the hymn ring down through the ages, affirming the spirit that animates the Lutheran faith today:

> And take they our life, goods, fame, child and wife.
> Let these all be gone, they yet have nothing won
> The Kingdom ours remaineth.

Author's Note

THE INSPIRATION FOR *LUTHER'S FORTRESS* LIES IN MY 2008 book, *Defenders of the Faith*, which covers the period of European history from 1520 to 1536. In that age of memorable patriarchs and potentates, Luther's impact on history surpasses them all.

In writing *Defenders of the Faith*, I found myself utterly captivated by the great Reformer: his personality, his courage, his rebellion, the drama of his life, his passion and his honesty, his grace and his coarseness, his wit and humor, and his flaws. And I was struck by the modern relevance of his story. His unflinching self-examination of his own sexuality led him to reject celibacy for the priesthood and challenge his vows as an Augustinian monk. This has resonance for current troubles in the Catholic Church. The difficulty of holding together his fragile movement against the challenges of more radical and less impressive men while he was in exile at the Wartburg, invoked for me memories of the fragile political movements in modern times. His struggle to define what he believed and what he rejected in the prevailing doctrines of the day reflects my own spiritual quest.

His story has another connection to my past work. In my 1994 biography of Galileo, I argued that Galileo's demonstration of a dynamic universe with the evidence of his telescope changed the course of human events forever and marked the divide between ancient and modern history. The same can be said of Luther's rebellion. (In a curious way Galileo and Luther shared similar personality traits; both were courageous, wry, contemptuous, brilliant skeptics of established authority.) Authentic Protestantism began with Luther and not with Henry VIII, for Henry's break with Rome was a vanity relating to the succession of his dynasty—and to his lust—whereas Luther's revolt was organic, stemming directly from the abuses of the church and from his fundamental disagreement with church dogma. This led to a wholly new and permanent way for Christians to worship.

For the storyteller in me Luther's sequestration at the Wartburg Castle was a gift, for it marked the most passionate, most productive, and most profound period of his incredible life. His translation of the New Testament is a literary masterpiece that set the standard for high German to this day. His life alone in captivity led him to confirm, consolidate, and lend completeness to his new doctrine, most especially his fundamental, defining concept of justification by faith alone. His Lenten lectures upon his return from exile to Wittenberg provide a triumphant, transformational moment in his life and work.

My focus on the Wartburg saga began with a visit to that castle in the summer of 2009 for a piece in the *Washington Post* that followed the publication of *Defenders of the Faith*. It was my good fortune to arrive there when an exhibition on Luther's translation of the Bible was on display. In the spring of 2014 I returned to the Wartburg for a deeper look and had a long, useful conversation with Dr. Jutta Krauss, the person responsible for historical research for the Wartburg Foundation and the one who has the overwhelming task of planning for an estimated four hundred thousand pilgrims to the Wartburg in 2017. I took note, with some disappointment, that in 2014, unlike 2009, the ink stain on the wall of Luther's cell had been removed, as if the managers were not really sure after all that

Luther had thrown his ink pot at the Devil. Dr. Krauss punctured the fun by stating that the ink pot myth was first mentioned in the seventeenth century.

Also in that same 2014 trip I spent days in Wittenberg at the Lutherhaus, the best repository of Luther materials and artifacts and the epicenter for the 2017 planning. The Lutherhaus now occupies the Augustinian monastery where Luther was a monk and which became Luther's family house after his return from his Wartburg exile and his marriage to Katarina von Bora. It is now a UNESCO World Heritage site. There I had extensive talks with the director, Dr. Stefan Rhein; the chief curator, Dr. Mirko Gutjahr; and Dr. Astrid Mühlmann, the lead organizer for the extensive federal and state government involvement in planning for the October 2017 Jubilee.

"All the world is coming to Wittenberg in 2017," I remarked to Dr. Rhein.

"Yes," he replied. "We hope, and we fear."

In the dark days of East German communism, Wittenberg was a gray, grimy, heavily polluted place. But since reunification in 1990, its stolid houses have been scrubbed and freshly painted in pastel colors, its cobblestone streets repaired, and its famous castle church, with its famous iron door, readied for the hordes of tourists. In the spring of 2014 the town was one big construction zone. The town church was closed, its twin towers invisible and encased in scaffolding. The thirteenth-century castle of Frederick the Wise was completely wrapped in plastic as if Christo had been here. Its outside skin was being dried and desalinated, before it was to receive a new coating of stucco. The cost of Wittenberg's face lift was put at something over 100 million euros. The goal was to restore the town to the way it looked in its most glorious period, around 1892 under Prussian rule.

In both Wittenberg and Eisenach, the town below the Wartburg castle, the relationship of Luther's theology to the Nazis is never far from mind. Far from avoiding this sensitive subject, the organizers of the Luther Jubilee seemed eager to address the dark sides of Luther. That Hitler and the Nazis seized on Luther's anti-Semitic writings is undeniable. Hitler mentioned the Reformer in *Mein Kampf* and in his speech to the Nürnberg Reichsparteitag in 1923. After Hitler rose to power, Lutheran officials endorsed him and the National Socialist Party. In 1933 the Lutheran church started using the Arian paragraphs, which prohibited anyone related to a Jew from working in the church. In the permanent exhibition at the Lutherhaus is a photograph of Nazi flags draping the rafters of the castle church in 1933.

And high on the southwest corner of Wittenberg's town church, where Luther gave over two thousand sermons, including his triumphant Invocavit Sermons in March 1522, there is a shocking fourteenth-century sculpture depicting the so-called *Judenseu* or Jewish swine. It portrays Jews suckling the paps of a pig, and their rabbi smelling its backside. In ancient times this appalling carving was meant to discourage Jews from settling in the town. The slur is scarcely confined to Wittenberg, but still exists on churches and public buildings throughout Germany, as well as in Austria, France, Belgium, and Switzerland. This symbol of profane folk art was revived in the Nazi period, inspiring the slander "Jewish pig."

In the year after he returned from the Wartburg, Luther took a sympathetic view toward the Jews. In his essay "That Jesus Christ Was Born a Jew," he defended the Jews and criticized Christians who treated Jews "as if they were dogs." There is evidence that he hoped to persuade Jews to leave Judaism and join his new brand of Christianity. But in this he was to be disappointed, and in time his view of Judaism soured.

Toward the end of his life, Luther turned passionately in the opposite direction, publishing two viciously anti-Semitic pamphlets, *On Jews and Their Lies* and *Vom Schem Hamphoras*. In the former he wrote that Jews were a "base, whoring people, that is, no people of God. Their boast of lineage, circumcision, and law must be accounted as filth." They were full of the "Devil's feces . . . which they wallow in like swine." He called the synagogue a "defiled bride, yes, an incorrigible whore and an evil slut" and argued that their synagogues and schools should be set on fire, their prayer books destroyed, rabbis forbidden to preach, homes razed, and property confiscated.

In 1988, fifty years after *Kristallnacht*—the beginning of the violent Nazi pogrom against the Jews—the town council of Wittenberg commissioned an antidote, a modern sculpture for the base of the church's southwest corner beneath the *Judenseu*. It has four square metal plates covering up a Christian cross and pointing to the fact that six million Jews were murdered under the sign of the cross. Its inscription acknowledges guilt and warns the viewer never to forget history. Additionally, in Wittenberg as well as in Eisenach and towns and cities across Germany, the Holocaust is personalized with small, square gold plaques marking the houses of victims, citing the day they were deported, the camp to which they were sent, and the day they were murdered.

In the shadow of the Wartburg castle, Eisenach has its own historical burden. During the Nazi period it was home to an especially nasty Lutheran bishop named Martin Sasse, who regularly preached against the Jews in the church on the town square. Shortly after the *Kristallnacht*, this evangelical minister published an edition of Luther's writings, entitled *Martin Luther on the Jews: Away with Them!* "On November 10, 1938, on Luther's birthday," he wrote in the introduction, "the synagogues were burning in Germany." The German people ought to heed these words of Martin Luther, "the greatest anti-Semite of his time." Bishop Sasse was associated with an institute in Eisenach called the Institute for Research and Removal of Jewish Influence on Church Life, whose "research" included the daunting task of removing all Jewish references from the Bible. The lyrics of Lutheran hymns were changed to remove the reference to Zion, and in the title page of newly issued Bibles, the famous, love-inspiring Luther rose was replaced with a swastika.

In my talk with Dr. Rhein at the Lutherhaus I mentioned to him
how in the run-up to the millennial year of 2000 the Roman Catholic Church had announced a process of "historical purification" in
which the divine institution promised to revisit the dark parts of
its history as a kind of spiritual cleansing. It began with the Galileo
case and was supposed to move on to the treatment of the heretic Jan Huss and then to the Spanish Inquisition. But the reconsideration of Galileo bogged down and never went deeper into other
dark corners. After thirteen years of reconsideration the church was
loathe to acknowledge anything more in the Galileo case than that
"mistakes were made," but it did not specify who made the mistakes.
The noble process of historical purification never moved on to the
case of Jan Huss or the horror of the Spanish Inquisition.

Might not the same thing happen to the Lutheran purification?
I asked.

Luther had been right about many important things, Dr. Rhein
replied, but he was not right about everything. There is no concept
of infallibility in Lutheranism, for reformation is an ongoing, dynamic, endless process. On my pad, he scratched the Latin mantra
of the Lutheran church, *Ecclesia semper reformanda*, "the church always reforming."

"We Protestants are more apt to admit our mistakes than are the
Catholics," he quipped.

If Wittenberg was selected as the hub for the 2017 Luther Jubilee, Worms is permanently memorialized as the place where his
movement metamorphosed from ecclesiastical to political. Eighty
percent of the town was destroyed in World War II and hastily rebuilt in the 1950s, but there are still remnants of the Middle Ages.
On the site of the old medieval moat stands the largest Reformation
monument in the world. Designed by Ernst Riefschel and erected in
1868, the fascinating statue of Luther presents the Reformer in a heroic stance, one foot in front of the other, above two victims of the
Inquisition's fire, Jan Huss and Savonarola. The joke around Worms

is that one more step, and Luther would have tumbled into the same funeral pyre as they.

Like planets in different orbits, the Imperial Cathedral of St. Peter in Worms, consecrated in 1110, stands opposite the spare Reformation church. (The town is split roughly in half between Catholics and Protestants.) On the back wall of the rebuilt evangelical church is a modern frieze of Luther standing at attention before Charles V. I asked the church's longtime pastor about how he saw the five hundredth anniversary of the Ninety-Five Theses. The event had to be clear-eyed and honest about the darker aspects of Luther's life, he said, especially the Reformer's negative attitude toward Turks and Mennonites and his vitriol toward Jews, as well as his incitement to the slaughter of peasants in the so-called Peasants War in 1524–1525. To do otherwise, said the pastor, "would be a sort of idolatry." Still, it gnawed at him that the Roman Catholic ban on Luther "and all his followers" is still in effect.

Across the street, I asked the Catholic provost of the Worms cathedral about this. Wasn't it time, in the interest of ecumenicalism, after five hundred years, that the excommunication of Luther and the ban on Lutheranism be lifted?

"The time to lift the ban has not yet come," he replied. "It is too early."

ACKNOWLEDGMENTS

In the more than two years it took to write *Luther's Fortress*, I again relied on the prodigious resources of the Woodrow Wilson International Center for Scholars with which I've had a long association. The head librarian there, Janet Spikes, was eager to help with my many requests as she has done with such good cheer for me on previous books. Over the course of the writing I had help from five bright and enthusiastic interns: Katia Esarey, Lukas Lademann, Sam Benka, Kellan Klaus, and Michael Held. Katia, Lukas, Sam, and Michael are all fluent German speakers, an immense help to me for the more esoteric searches in sixteenth-century German. Kellan, a cheerful religious studies major from Louisiana, was very helpful as a sounding board for the larger context and meaning of Luther's theology. In addition, I had help at the Library of Congress in Washington, the Lauringer Library at Georgetown University, the German Historical Institute in Washington, the Peabody Library in Baltimore, and the library at the Lutheran Theological Seminary in Gettysburg, Pennsylvania.

In Germany, as mentioned, I got wonderful help from Dr. Stefan Rhein, Dr. Mirko Gutjahr, and Astrid Mühlmann at the Lutherhaus in Wittenberg, and Dr. Jutta Krauss at the Wartburg. In Eisenach I was guided around, in both 2009 and 2014, by the wonderful and engaging Alexandra Husemeyer, who frequently plays Luther's wife, Katharina von Bora, in local productions. And I'm grateful for the hospitality of the Eisenacher Hof and its lively owner, Udo Winkels, who plays a feisty, hilarious Martin Luther at his hotel's raucous Lutherstuben almost every Saturday night. In Leipzig, on the subject of the Leipzig Trade Fair in 1522, I had a most useful contact with Dr. Philipp Rössner, an economic historian who is a specialist in the monetary history of Luther's time.

In Worms I wish to thank Rev. Harald Storch, the longtime pastor of the Evangelical Reformation Church, and Monsignor Engelbert Priess, the provost of the Imperial Cathedral of St. Peter, for their patience and wisdom.

Finally, I am especially fortunate in this work to have as my agent Markus Hoffmann, a native German and the son of a Methodist minister. Markus accompanied me on my trip to Wittenberg and the Wartburg in April 2014. His comments on the manuscript, as in previous projects, were wise and helpful. Even more important was the fine hand of my splendid editor at Basic Books, Alex Littlefield. His incisive comments and suggestions on the text, sometimes suggestive of the surgeon's scalpel and repairing thread, have improved this book immensely.

Selected Bibliography

Primary Sources

Luther, Martin. *D. Martin Luthers Werke: Kritische Gesamtausgabe.* 4 vols. Weimar: H. Böhlau, 1883.
———. *Luther's Works.* 54 vols. General editors Jaroslav Pelikan (vols. 1–30) and Helmut T. Lehman (vols. 31–54). St. Louis: Concordia; Philadelphia: Fortress, 1955–1976.
———. *Martin Luther's Christmas Book.* Edited by Roland H. Bainton. Minneapolis: Augsburg, 1948.

Secondary Sources

Atkinson, James. *The Trial of Luther.* New York: Stein and Day, 1971.
Audin, M. *The History of the Life, Writings, and Doctrines of Luther.* London: Dolman, 1854.
Bainton, Roland H. *Here I Stand: The Life of Martin Luther.* Nashville, TN: Abingdon, 1950.
Beard, Charles. *Martin Luther and the Reformation in Germany Until the Close of the Diet of Worms.* London: K. Paul, Trench, 1889.

Bender, Harold S. "The Zwickau Prophets, Thomas Muntzer, and the Anabaptists." *Mennonite Quarterly Review* 27 (1953).

Betten, Francis S., S.J. "The Cartoon in Luther's Warfare Against the Church." *Catholic Historical Review* 11 (July 1925).

Brandi, Karl. *The Emperor Charles V: The Growth and Destiny of a Man and of a World Empire.* Translated by C. V. Wedgwood. Atlantic Highlands, NJ: Humanities, 1980.

Brecht, Martin. *Martin Luther: Shaping and Defining the Reformation.* Philadelphia: Fortress, 1985.

Bluhm, Heinz. *Martin Luther: Creative Translator.* St. Louis, MO: Concordia, 1965.

Burckhardt, Jacob. *The Civilization of the Renaissance in Italy.* New York: Harper, 1958.

Camerarius, Joachim. *De Vita Phillippi Melanchthonis.* 1777.

Catholic Encyclopedia. Vol. 9. New York: Encyclopedia Press, 1917.

Christensen, Carl C. "Luther and the Woodcuts to the 1534 Bible." *Lutheran Quarterly* (2005).

Clair, Colin. *A History of European Printing.* London: Academic Press, 1976.

Coignet, Clarisse. *Francis the First and His Times.* New York: Scribner and Welford, 1889.

Creighton, M. A. *History of the Papacy from the Great Schism to the Sack of Rome.* Vol. 6. New York: Longmans, Green, 1897.

Defoe, Daniel. *The Political History of the Devil.* London: T. Warner, 1726.

Dickens, A. G. *The German Nation and Martin Luther.* New York: Harper & Row, 1974.

Dies Buch in aller Junge, Hand und Herzen. 2009. Catalogue for the exhibition on Luther's translation work at the Wartburg Castle.

Doernberg, Edwin. *Henry VIII and Luther: An Account of Their Personal Relations.* London: Barrie and Rockliff, 1961.

Eisenstein, Elizabeth L. *The Printing Revolution in Early Modern Europe.* New York: Cambridge University Press, 2005.

Erikson, Erik H. *Young Man Luther.* New York: W. W. Norton, 1958.

Friedenthal, Richard. *Luther: His Life and Times.* Translated by John Nowell. New York: Harcourt, Brace, Jovanovich, 1970.

Fudge, Thomas A. "Incest and Lust in Luther's Marriage: Theology and Morality in Reformation Polemics." *Sixteenth Century Journal* 34, no. 2 (Summer 2003): 319–345.

Gregorovius, Ferdinand. *History of the City of Rome in the Middle Ages.* Vol. 8. London: G. Bell & Sons, 1912.

Grimm, Harold. *Martin Luther as Preacher.* Columbus, OH: Lutheran Book Concern, 1929.

Grisar, Hartmann, S.J. *Martin Luther: His Life and Work.* St. Louis, MO: B. Herder, 1930.

Gritsch, Eric W. *The Wit of Martin Luther.* Minneapolis, MN: Fortress, 2006.

Guicciardini, Francesco. *The History of Italy.* New York: Macmillan, 1969.

Hempsall, David. "On Martin Luther and the Sorbonnne, 1519–21." *Bulletin of the Institute of Historical Research* 46, no. 113 (May 1973).

Hendrix, Scott H. *Luther and the Papacy: Stages in a Reformation Conflict.* Philadelphia: Fortress, 1981.

Henry VIII. *Assertio Septem Sacramentorum or Defence of the Seven Sacraments.* New York: Benziger Brothers, 1908.

Hibbert, Christopher. *The House of Medici.* New York: William Morrow, 1975.

Kuhr, Olaf. "The Zwickau Prophets, the Wittenberg Disturbances, and Polemical Historiography." *Mennonite Quarterly Review* (April 1996).

Luther, Martin. *Luther's Christmas Sermons.* Translated by John Nicholas Lenker. Minneapolis, MN: Luther Press, 1908.

Mackinnon, James. *Luther and the Reformation.* London: Longmans, Green, 1929.

Manschreck, Clyde. *Melanchthon, Quiet Reformer*. Westport, CT: Greenwood, 1958.

Metzger, Bruce M. *The Bible in Translation*. Grand Rapids, MI: Baker Academic, 2001.

Mittmann, Roland. "Deutsche Sprachgeschichte." Institut für Linguistik, Universität Frankfurt, 2010.

More, Sir Thomas. *Responsio ad Lutherum*. Edited by John M. Headley. Translated by Sister Scholastica. *The Complete Works of St. Thomas More*, vol. 5. New Haven, CT: Yale University Press, 1969.

Mullet, Michael A. *Martin Luther*. London: Routledge, 2004.

Nello splendore mediceo Papa Leone X e Firenze. Edited by Nicoletta Baldini and Monica Bietti. Florence: Sillabe, 2013.

Neues Leipzigisches Geschicht Buch. Leipzig: Fachbuchverlag, 1990.

Nicolson, Adam. *God's Secretaries: The Making of the King James Bible*. New York: Harper Perennial, 2004.

Norlie, O. M., ed. *The Translated Bible, 1534–1934*. Philadelphia: United Lutheran, 1934.

Oberman, Heiko A. *Luther: Man Between God and the Devil*. New Haven, CT: Yale University Press, 1989.

Ozment, Steven. *The Serpent and the Lamb: Cranach, Luther, and the Making of the Reformation*. New Haven, CT: Yale University Press, 2011.

Pastor, Ludwig Freiherr von. *The History of the Popes: From the Close of the Middle Ages*. Vol. 8, edited by R. F. Kerr. St. Louis, MO: Herder, 1923–1969.

Pelikan, Jaroslav. *Luther the Expositor*. Philadelphia: Fortress, 1959.

Probst, Christopher J. *Demonizing the Jews: Luther and the Protestant Church in Nazi Germany*. Bloomington: Indiana University Press, 2012.

Robertson, William. *The History of the Reign of the Emperor Charles V*. London: Lippincott, 1904.

Roscoe, William. *The Life and Pontificate of Leo X*. 4 vols. London: Henry G. Bohn, 1853.

Rupp, E. Gordon. "Andreas Karlstadt and Reformation Puritanism." *Journal of Theological Studies* n.s. 10 (1959): 308–326.

Schaeffer, William B. "Luther's Invocavit Sermons of March 1522: A Pastoral Approach to Change and Controversy." Thesis. Lutheran Theological Seminary, Gettysburg, PA.

Schaff, Philip. *History of the Christian Church*. Peabody, MA: Hendrickson, 1996.

Smith, Preserved. "Luther's Development of the Doctrine of Justification by Faith Only." *Harvard Theological Review* (October 1913).

Strathern, Paul. *The Medici: Godfathers of the Renaissance*. London: Pimlico, 2005.

Strieder, Peter. *Albrecht Dürer: Paintings, Prints, Drawings*. New York: Abaris Books, 1989.

Stupperich, Robert. *Melanchthon*. London: Lutterworth, 1966.

Trinterud, L. J. "A Reappraisal of William Tyndale's Debt to Martin Luther." *Church History* (March 1962).

Vaughan, Herbert M. *The Medici Popes*. Port Washington, NY: Kennikat, 1971.

Verres, J. *Luther, an Historical Portrait*. London: Burns & Oates, 1884.

Waetzoldt, Wilhelm. *Dürer and His Times*. London: Phaidon, 1955.

Wylie, James. *The History of Protestantism*. London: Cassell, 1874.

INDEX

251